# CHRISTIANITY
## and the errors of Paul

NATHAN BEN RAGSHI

Harmony Publishing
Plot 8, Providence Street, Opposite Halifield School, Lekki Phase 1, Lagos, Nigeria.
+2347032212481
publish@harmonypublishing.com.ng


ISBN: 978-978-60691-5-9

# DEDICATION

*I dedicate this work to my brothers and sisters, Michael, Elizabeth, Nina, Miriam, Valerie and others the world over who do the will of the Father in Heaven to worship Him in Truth and Spirit. For such like you, the Father searches in the sacrifice of His Only Begotten Son Yahshua of Nazareth our Messiah. May your names be written in Heaven.*

# ACKNOWLEDGMENT

I thank You, O Father, Sustainer of heaven and earth, because You have hid many things from the wise so that they should not glory in their wisdom. You hid them also from the prudent so that they should not glory in their providence. You hid them also from imposters that their cozenage may be evident. Amazingly, you have revealed them to babes for so it looks good to you, that people may appreciate you further and know that it is not by force and not by muscle but by your Spirit.

Kudos to Rebekah, Wuraola, Oladunni, Olaitan and Milcah. You know how we do from Sabbath to Sabbath.

# PREFACE

This book is a deep discourse concerning scriptural Truth. At every level of understanding, no matter how shallow it may be, anyone with an idea of the narrative of Christianity can point to one or two ministers whom he or she considers a 'false prophet'. The Saviour warns every serious believer to 'beware of false prophets'. A serious believer should strive to understand what the Master is saying exactly and who a false prophet is from the Master's perspective and not from his/her opinion as a believer. Many charlatans, who claim to be apostles, prophets, ministers and men of God, go about deceiving people by faking miracles and engaging in witchcraft to exert crowd control. They are busy prophesying, praying long prayers and giving testimonies of unconfirmed miracles.

However, when you consider their interpretations of scripture, you find them skewed and false in essence. So, how can a man or woman who lacks understanding and proper interpretation of the text claim to work with the Spirit of the text? That is the threshold of false prophets. Nevertheless, you, as a believer, must understand how to apply thresholds to everyone and determine, by Yahshua Messiah's spirit, who a false prophet is.

Of course, there are levels of training and discipline that every serious disciple must undergo. Christianity has diverse sects and they are all different in their practices. Sometimes, one wonders what the cause of the discrepancy is. This kind of thought objectively leads one to the Truth. In the gospel according to Apostle John 18:37, he wrote,

***"Yahshua answered, Thou sayest that I am a king. To this end was I born, and for this cause came I into the world, that I should bear witness unto the truth. Everyone that is of the truth heareth my voice.***

Speaking for Yahshua Messiah as a Prophet or a Minister in any capacity is not about how much money one can extort from the gullible or how many people one can control. Rather, everything regarding preaching Yahshua Messiah is about demonstrating the Truth about Yahweh Elohim the Father and His only begotten Son through the Holy Scriptures of Truth beginning at the knowledge of the names of the Father and of His Son.

Proverbs 30:4, ***"Who hath ascended up into heaven, or descended? who hath gathered the wind in his fists? who hath bound the waters in a garment? who hath established all the ends of the earth? what is his name, and what is his son's name, if thou canst tell?"***

# TABLE OF CONTENTS

# INTRODUCTION

Nathan Ben Ragshs, a servant of Yahshua Messiah and a prophet of Yahshua Messiah in Verity, for the name and in the name of Yahshua Messiah – a letter to the ecclesia, which consists of every sincere believer who seeks to deify the Father of life in Truth and in Spirit through the only begotten Son of the Father.

Nathan Ben Ragshi, a servant and a prophet of Yahshua of Nazareth the Messiah. I was first a believer of Yahshua Messiah, then a follower and then a disciple before I was elevated to the high office of a prophet. The message in this book should present proof of this prophethood. Such confirmation and proof of prophethood should matter to every believer, adherent or practitioner of any faith that engages the service of prophets, most especially the Faith of Yahshua of Nazareth the Messiah.

# Chapter 1
# THE PROPHET

# WHO OR WHAT IS A PROPHET?

The Bible comprises mainly of the works of prophets even though it contains some works of scribes on historical records in the 'Old Testament'. Most of the Bible as a book contains the works of prophets. Meanwhile, in the 'New Testament', the most important parts are the works of the witnesses of the life and ministry of Yahshua of Nazareth, who Himself functioned in the office of a prophet before he was revealed as being the Messiah by his resurrection from the dead. It should, therefore, interest any believer or reader of the Bible to consider the content of this publication deeply.

The Master Yahshua Messiah taught us, as His disciples, many lessons of great importance. The teachings and lessons of Yahshua Messiah are of such importance because there are eternal consequences with regards to how they are handled. A believer in Yahshua Messiah believes that He is the only begotten Son of the Father and Creator of life and that the Father sent Yahshua Messiah to come into the world to save the world particularly those who believe him from eternal damnation.

This salvation is a massive topic on its own and it was prophesied by several prophets many years before the physical manifestation of the man Yahshua Messiah. When Yahshua of Nazareth began his ministry as the Messiah, He taught his disciples to understand that the prophecies of the prophets pointed to Himself as the Messiah. He also taught them how to understand the mechanism and operation of the salvation he came to accomplish for men so that those who believe in Him may obtain the salvation and benefit from it successfully.

In dealing with the sensitive issue of who a prophet is, we should begin at the foundation of the topic, which serves as the fundamental explanation and then progress accordingly.

The word "prophet", according to one English dictionary, is borrowed from the Greek word ***prophetes*** which means one who interprets the will of a god to humans.

In English, a Prophet is defined as;

1. One who utters divinely inspired revelations such as

    a. The writer of one of the prophetic books in the Bible

    b. One regarded by followers as the final authoritative revealer of God's will, i.e. Muhammad, the Prophet of Allah.

2. One gifted with more than ordinary spiritual and moral insight, i.e. an inspired poet

3. One who foretells future invents, i.e. a predictor

4. An effective or leading spokesman for a cause, doctrine, or group

5. In Christian Science, a spiritual seer

Now, the word 'prophet', according to the Chambers 20th Century Dictionary, is derived from the Greek word *prophetes* as mentioned already, which comes from the root word *'pro'* meaning 'for' and *'phanai'* meaning 'to speak'. Hence, the word 'prophet' originally means a spokesman or spokesperson of a deity (a god or goddess), i.e. one who proclaims a divine message, an inspired teacher or preacher, a psalmist or poet and also a foreteller, whether inspired or not. A prophet can also be a pioneer of a new theory, movement or doctrine.

From the definitions of the word 'prophet', we see that there are three (3) main groups of persons that can be correctly referred to as prophets. These three groups must be stated clearly so that no part of the discussion is unclear.

The three main groups of persons are;

1. A spokesman of a deity, and that includes a preacher, a teacher or a minister

2. An initiator of a new theory, cause, group or movement

3. A foreteller who tells or claims to tell what will happen in the future, whether by inspiration or not

As we proceed, we shall refer to the above grouping whenever we use the word prophet, if necessary, to determine what group of prophets we are referring to.

Now that we have established the meaning of the word 'prophet' from the English dictionary, we shall look into the Holy Scriptures to understand what it means when we find the word 'prophet' in the scriptures. That way, we can comprehend the master's intent when he warned his followers to 'beware of false prophets', being a part of the inspiration for this book.

As we look into the scriptures to examine the word 'prophet' and those who rightly stand in that office, we must use our understanding, and prayerfully so, so we can grasp every minute but necessary detail concerning the subject. That is the only way we can have a profound comprehension of who a prophet is and thereby we can detect, decipher and determine who a false prophet is, according to the Master.

The first time the word 'prophet' is mentioned in the Scriptures, it was used by the Almighty Elohim himself. By the way, at this point, we should know that the Scriptures belong to the Israelites because it was committed to them and they speak the Hebrew tongue, whether in ancient or more recent forms. Meanwhile, we became familiar with the Scriptures in their translation into the English language.

It is improper to translate the work of a culture or people without recourse to the owners. Such an action will only produce endless errors and mistranslations. These errors are observable in many translated versions of the Bible because the Israelites or Jews were not considered or consulted, especially in the so-called 'New Testament' scriptures.

The Almighty Elohim first used the word 'prophet' to qualify Abraham, whom Elohim also called His friend. To this day, he (Abraham) is believed to be the father of our faith. This is recorded in the book of Genesis thus;

> ***"Now therefore restore the man his wife; for he is a Prophet***
>
> ***And he shall pray for thee and thou shall live."*** Gen 20:7

The scripture records that Elohim spoke these words in a dream to a man called Abimelech, who was then king of Gerar. This event happened when

Abraham journeyed to Kadesh, the Southern country in his time, and sojourned in the town called Gerar. The king of Gerar wanted to take his wife Sarah because she was beautiful and also because Abraham had introduced her to the king as his sister, which was somewhat true.

Elohim warned King Abimelech of Gerar in a dream to return the woman Sarah to her husband Abraham or face the death penalty. He complied immediately and returned the woman to her husband. I had to present the details of the event so that you the reader can know why Elohim spoke to Abimelech and called Abraham a prophet.

The Prophet is like an office or an instrument that Elohim uses to send His messages to people and also to reveal His plan for the present and the future. A prophet is chosen and ordained by Elohim Himself. A prophet or the office of the prophet is not established by knowledge acquisition or having a specific background.

In fact, Elohim has not revealed the requirements He uses to choose and ordain prophets. This is unlike the office of a priest or even a king which is hereditary or subject to the choice of men. That a man is a prophet does not make his son a prophet or his wife a prophetess.

This undefined process of choosing and ordaining prophets by Elohim makes it very easy for liars and eccentric people to rise and proclaim themselves as prophets. They deceive many ignorant souls and lead them to perdition, which already is the lot and judgment of false prophets.

By precept and example, Elohim made it clear that one who will be king will be ceremonially anointed. The same goes for the priest;

> *"These are the names of the sons of Aaron, the priests which*
> *Were anointed, whom he consecrated to minister in the*
> *Priest's office."* Numb 3v:3 (HNB)

Also, concerning Saul the king, the scripture records as follows;

> *"Samuel also said to Saul, Yahweh sent me to anoint thee*
> *To be king over His people, over Israel: now therefore*

> ***Harken thou unto the voice of the words of Yahweh.*** 1Sam15:1
> (HNB)

The point in our emphasis is that, unlike the election of kings and priests, the election of a prophet is done directly by Elohim. Also, the rules of selecting a prophet are unknown to any man.

Concerning the office of a prophet, let us consider what Elohim states in the scripture. Elohim made the pronouncement in the scripture below to resolve an argument about the office of His servant Moses. Hence, we must consider the details carefully, point by point, as this is the foundation of the revelation of this publication.

> ***"And Yahweh came down in the pillar of cloud, and stood***
> ***In the door of the meeting tent and called Aaron and Miriam:***
> ***And they both came forth. And He said, Hear now My Words:***
> ***If there be a prophet among you, I Yahweh will make Myself***
> ***Known to him in a vision, and will speak unto him in a dream."***
> Num. 12:5-6 (HNB)

The above scripture is the direct word of Elohim Yahweh, the Elohim of Israel, which He spoke when Miriam, the sister of Moses, was trying to convince their brother Aaron the priest to join her rebellion against Moses the servant of Yahweh Elohim. Needless to say Yahweh Elohim punished her for that rebellion with leprosy.

Moses, who, according to the word of Yahweh Elohim, was clearly higher in office than a prophet, had to intercede for Miriam to be forgiven by Yahweh Elohim. She was healed after seven days, and after this incident, she became very humble and respectful to Moses.

That incident allowed Yahweh Elohim to explain to all how He operates and commissions His prophets, which is strictly through visions and dreams. We must remember this point as we continue in the discussion.

Yahweh spoke directly, and not by the mouth of any prophet or priest, that he will reveal himself to a prophet through dreams and visions. Indeed, we find throughout the recorded scriptures that Yahweh continued to operate with his prophets in this manner. Also, he gave them an understanding heart, wisdom and revelation concerning the dreams and visions he showed them until the manifestation and revelation of His Messiah.

Having established the medium of Elohim's communication with a prophet, let us consider how the people of Yahweh (the Israelites after the flesh) considered a prophet. Originally, the Israelites referred to a prophet as a "seer" as he was supposed to see visions directly from Yahweh or indirectly as a dream. We see the record that men of Yahweh, who received visions from Yahweh, were called seers in the scriptures;

> *"And when they were come to the land of Zuph, Saul said*
>
> *To his servant that was with him, come, let us return; lest*
>
> *My father leave caring for the asses and take thought for us.*
>
> *And he said to him, behold now, there is in this city a man*
>
> *Of Elohim, and he is an honorable man; all that he saith cometh*
>
> *Surely to pass; now let us go thither peradventure he can shew*
>
> *Us our way that we should go"* 1Sam. 9:5-6 (HNB)

And then…

> *"(Beforetime in Israel, when a man went to enquire of Elohim,*
>
> *Thus he spake, come, let us go to the Seer; for he that is now.*
>
> *Called a Prophet was beforetime called a Seer.)"* 1Sam. 9:9

With the scriptural facts we have garnered so far, we can establish a more incontrovertible fact that a true prophet of Yahweh Elohim is a seer of visions and a dreamer of dreams. The Hebrew word used for a man of Elohim, who was a seer of vision, is Ra'ah which means 'to see, to look on, to see visions'. Meanwhile, the man of Elohim who got revelations through dreams was called Choseh (in Hebrew), i.e. a gazer or beholder of visions. The word 'choseh' is from the Hebrew word 'chazah' which is to gaze and perceive. It is also translated as stargazer in Isaiah 47:13. Fundamentally, Ra'ah refers to a man of Elohim who sees more clearly and completely than Choseh.

Now, let us consider the other uses of the word 'prophet' as seen in scripture and see where it is used without referring to an actual seer of visions and dreamer of dreams. When used for a man of Elohim who did not see visions or receive dreams from Elohim, the word 'prophet' is interpreted from the Hebrew word 'Nabi' which means to foretell and declare future events.

This foretelling of future events was not seen in a vision or dream as in the case of seers and dreamers considered earlier. Rather, these just speak by inspiration, sometimes as prayers and more often as predictions. These predictions were more often conditional. These inspirational predictions were more like a spiritual function instigated and operated by the Holy Spirit of Elohim while those who made the utterances did so as they were led by the Spirit. This office was later described in the revelations to the Church of Messiah, under the New Covenant, as the gift and function of the Holy Spirit called the gift of prophecy or prophesying.

Prophecy or prophesying is the utterance of divinely inspired and prophetic words. The utterance may be about the present, the past, but more often, the future. It is archaic and grammatically wrong now to equate prophecy with or refer to prophesying as preaching, expounding or interpreting the Scriptures publicly.

Although it is now obsolete in the English language to refer to prophecy or prophesying as preaching due to the redefining of the word in English, all such interpretations have always been scripturally wrong even as the word of Elohim remains the same and abides forever.

The operation of the Kingdom of Heaven on earth through the office of prophets by Yahweh ended with the revelation of Yahshua Messiah as the only Begotten Son of Yahweh. This is what the author of the letter to the Hebrews in Hebrews 1:1-2 means when he said;

*"Elohim, who at sundry times and in divers manners spake in time past unto the fathers by the prophets, Hath in these last days spoken unto us by his Son, whom he hath appointed heir of all things, by whom also he made the worlds."*

The Master Yahshua of Nazareth made it clear that there has been a shift in the operation of the Kingdom of Heaven on earth from the advent of John the Baptist. We find this in the Gospel according to Luke in Luke 16:16; *"The law and the prophets were until John: since that time the kingdom of God is preached, and every man treats it with contempt."* (HNB)

To a large extent, every true believer and disciple is a prophet and an evangelist of the Master. Noteworthy is the fact that among the Prophets, evangelists and believers, there are the Elders and the Advanced in the Faith, and there are the infants and toddlers in the Faith also. Conversely, there are reprobates also, as well as there are traitors, enemies and saboteurs of the Truth.

Believers must assess their faith occasionally to sincerely determine if they are still in the Faith and standing on the Truth or if they have become reprobates concerning the Faith. Therefore, let he who thinks he is standing be careful and be sure that he has not fallen already.

As a person born into Christianity and being inclined to Truth-seeking, I continued to assess my Christian faith objectively. I soon realized that Christianity is a religion that is totally feigned yet unjustly and wrongly affiliated with the Truth. This makes it more difficult to determine its authenticity and makes it more dangerous to the Truth than Islam, which openly opposes the Truth rather than being affiliated with the same.

In the Faith or religion of Israel, specifically that of the Jews which is sometimes called Judaism, Christianity is the exact allegorical manifestation of the worship of the Golden Molten Calf fashioned by Aaron the Priest and brother of Moses in Exodus 32:4: *"And he received them at their hand, and fashioned it with a graving tool after he had made it a molten calf: and they said, These be thy Elohim, O Israel, which brought thee up out of the land of Egypt".*

Christianity is also the allegorical manifestation of the religion of the Golden Calves made by King Jeroboam the Son of Nebat, King of Israel in 1Kings12:28:

*"Whereupon the king took counsel, and made two calves of gold, and said unto them, It is too much for you to go up to Jerusalem: behold thy Elohim, O Israel, which brought thee up out of the land of Egypt."*

In both aforementioned cases, we observe that the idols, which were fabricated and were falsely made to be objects of worship, were affiliated with the 'Truth'. The Truth being the Fact and reality of the Exodus of the children of Israel from the land of Egypt.

Exodus 32:4: ***... And they said, These be thy gods, O Israel, which brought thee up out of the land of Egypt.***

1 Kings 12:28 ***...Behold thy gods, O Israel, which brought thee up out of the land of Egypt.***

Coming out of the land of Egypt is true, but the statement about the idols being the power that effected the emigration is false, if we consider it using the Boolean algebra of mathematical logic.

Of course, if we consider the properties of creation starting from our earth in relationship to our sun, the moon, our solar system and our galaxy, we discover that if there is a creator, the creator is more scientific in operation in terms of Mathematics, Physics, Chemistry and Biology rather than artistic or linguistic. In fact, one of the leading scientists and astrophysicists of our time Neil deGrasse Tyson stated that **"Math is the language of the Universe"**.

That is why the most reliable and effective understanding of the Word of the Scriptures of Truth contained in the Holy Bible is by the application of Mathematical operations, including mathematical logic of the Boolean expression which indicates the results of any condition as True or False.

It is clear that the statement "These be thy gods, O Israel, which brought thee up out of the land of Egypt" is false considering the function "and" in logical conjunction.

Also, in Christianity, the main character is given the name "Jesus'. However, in fact and truth, that is not the name the man that Christians refer to bore while he walked on the earth. When the man's original name is transliterated from Hebrew, which is His native language (being a Jew) to English (the present language of the Bible), the correct resultant name is Yahoshua, which is contracted to Yahshua.

Let's not forget that the Israelites speak Hebrew and the term given to the Saviour King they were and are still expecting is pronounced Mashiach in Hebrew, which is transliterated correctly to Messiah in English.

The name **'Jesus'** is, therefore, a fabrication used to replace the original name **'Yahshua'** many years after the fact of his life on earth. Also, the word **"Christ"** is an interpolation and a replacement for the word **"Messiah"**.

Using the Boolean expression, it is clear that this statement as follows is false: "Jesus Christ was killed on the cross outside Jerusalem about 2000 years ago, was buried in a sepulchre and rose again on the third day". This is because no Jewish man ever bore the name 'Jesus' and 'Christ' is not the right transliteration of the Hebrew word Mashiach or Messiah. This fundamental ideology and statement of Christianity is, therefore, false, logically speaking.

The falsity of the fundamental ideology of Christianity can and will be debated and disputed by the leaders of Christianity, using all manner of apologetics and counter-apologetics. However, this is just a little digression and not the focus of this publication.

It's interesting to note that the most widely distributed version of the English Bible which is the King James Version (KJV) has been revised, edited and republished as the "Restored Name King James Version" (RNKJV). This means the original names of the main characters of the Bible have been restored and the fabricated names removed. Certainly, there have been many other versions of the Bible where these corrections to altered and replaced Hebrew names have been made even more elaborately.

Presently, Christianity has Seven (7) main branches and about thirty-three thousand (33,000) different denominations worldwide. This is due to different ideologies, readings and understanding of the texts of the Bible. This has resulted in so many sects and congregations—a situation that is in contrast with the original understanding given by the one and only Master and founder of the Faith that all the different sects of adherents purport to follow and deify.

The origin of this deviation and departure from the original understanding of the Faith and the resultant diversity among the adherents are parts of the reasons and motivations for this publication.

Christianity is supposed to be a Faith and not a religion. One may wonder about the difference between a Faith and a religion. By revelation, I have defined **Faith** as the '**proper understanding of what is believed**', while religion remains a **"set of beliefs and practices"**. This means that without understanding, whatever is believed is mere belief. Meanwhile, a belief can be right or wrong, and what is believed can always be true or false.

This position is true and reflected in the scriptural record of the sayings of the wise king Solomon in Proverbs 4:7; *"Wisdom is supreme. Get wisdom. Yes, though it costs all your possessions, get understanding"*.

The understanding of a belief or what is believed turns the belief into faith. In mathematical parlance, a belief is a fixed value. For example, we believe that God created the universe but the understanding is variable in value as in deep or shallow, which results in little or great Faith as the case may be.

As stated already, the main character and Master of the Faith, belief or religion of Christianity (as the case may be) is a Jewish man whose proper name is Yahshua. This name is a Hebrew name commonly borne by Jewish men from ancient times. Also, the Master of the Faith, by instruction, is not distinguished from other namesakes of his by surname or by his earthly father's name but rather by the town in which he grew up — Nazareth.

The designation, therefore, is that **'Yahshua of Nazareth is the Messiah'**. This statement will sit reasonably well with and make sense to any Jewish person whether or not they believe it. However, to tell a Jewish or Hebrew person that **Jesus of Nazareth is Christ** is nonsensical at least to a Jewish person who believes the Hebrew Scriptures.

This man Yahshua of Nazareth claimed to be the Messiah of the Jews and Israelites. For this, He was found guilty of blasphemy and executed outside Jerusalem at the stakes of Golgotha. He was condemned because the religious leadership of the Jews at that time felt that He (Yahshua of Nazareth) did not meet the criteria to qualify as the Messiah they had been awaiting since their sojourn in the land of Egypt.

After this man Yahshua of Nazareth was executed and confirmed dead, he was buried in a sepulchre. After three days and three nights in the sepulchre, he resurrected in his physical body. He then showed himself alive to his

Apostles and disciples before he ascended into heaven. Before he left, he made a clear promise to return much later with mighty angels and glorious power to rule the world and judge both the living and the dead.

Several years before the trial, execution, burial, resurrection and ascension of Yahshua Messiah, he had a few thousand followers due to the genuine miracles he performed. Among those followers, he had disciples who were interested in his teachings, ministry and purpose.

From among his many disciples, he elected twelve men whom he labelled and designated as Apostles. These Apostles are the very foundations of the Faith or Belief in Yahshua as the Messiah. They are the witnesses of his earthly life, teachings, miracles, trial, suffering, execution, burial and resurrection. He chose them to be his most intimate witnesses.

Without being a physical witness of the earthly life and teachings of this Man Yahshua Messiah, it is impossible to be an apostle of His. When Yahshua Messiah elected the twelve apostles, he presented them to the disciples and other followers so that they could be known and distinguished as the Apostles appointed by the Master Yahshua Messiah himself.

These twelve Apostles are also an allegorical manifestation of the twelve sons of Jacob, the patriarch of the nation whose name was changed to Israel. Hence, there cannot be more than twelve Apostles forever just as there cannot be more than twelve sons of Jacob forever.

Of course, one of the twelve Apostles, Judah Iscariot Ben Simon, who betrayed the Master to the Jewish leaders who condemned the Master and ensured they executed Him, was considered as lost and his office was declared vacant just like Joseph (one of the twelve sons of Jacob) was considered dead. Eventually, Joseph was replaced by his two sons Manasseh and Ephraim just as Judah Iscariot was replaced by two options chosen from among the other disciples that had followed the Master throughout his earthly ministry — Acts 1:23: ***"And they appointed two, Joseph called Barsabas, who was surnamed Justus, and Matthias. Mathias was chosen by prayers and casting lots"***.

The point here is that any other person who was not appointed by the Master, and most importantly, who did not walk with the Master physically nor heard His words and teachings while He was on earth, cannot claim to be an Apostle of the Messiah.

This truth is affirmed in Revelation 21:14; ***"And the wall of the city had twelve foundations, and in them the names of the twelve apostles of the Lamb"***.

This verse talks about the heavenly Jerusalem that is to come and permanently establishes the fact of twelve Apostles and no more than twelve apostles forever.

Strangely, after these twelve appointed Apostles, some people mindlessly call themselves Apostles of the Faith of Yahshua Messiah. However, with this understanding of the statutory twelve Apostles, it is clear that such people are false. In essence, they are imposters who are destitute of the truth and understanding of the Faith. They are more easily spotted than other imposters in their category which includes false prophets, false teachers and even false brethren.

Some of these imposters use the terms major and minor Apostles to distinguish themselves from the twelve true Apostles. I would rather and any serious believer should also use the term true and false Apostles instead of the ambiguous major and minor Apostles, and I stand to be corrected. The idea and accompanying problems of claiming to be an Apostle of the Messiah without seeing or physically walking with the Master and Messiah started with a prominent character in the Bible known as Paul.

Paul called himself an Apostle or maybe the use of the title was the making of the translators of his writings. Whatever the case may be, he Paul being called an apostle is an error and a lie. An Apostle must have seen the Messiah and followed Him in His mortal tabernacle as a man listened to His teachings, witnessed His miracles, suffering and death by crucifixion, and seen Him after His resurrection in His celestial tabernacle to have a good recollection of His teachings and His purpose. An Apostle must be personally appointed and named by the Master as an Apostle in the presence of other disciples. Paul does not meet any of these criteria.

I studied the works of Paul for many years with prayers and dedication before I received the revelation and understanding I am sharing in this write-up. This revelation came to me through a Spirit which I will call the Spirit of Truth and correctly so. After all, the term "Holy Spirit" has been thoroughly abused by Christians despite the Master's warning in Matthew 12:31; *"Wherefore I say unto you, All manner of sin and blasphemy shall be forgiven unto men: but the blasphemy against the Holy Spirit shall not be forgiven unto men"*.

When Christians lie, speak errors and falsehoods and mention the Holy Spirit as the source, they do not take into cognizance that lying on, about or concerning the Holy Spirit is an unforgivable sin in this age and in the age to come.

Back to the matter, I use the term Spirit of Truth rather than Holy Spirit. It is exactly the same spirit though but I use the term 'Spirit of Truth' because you cannot be in error or speak falsely and claim that the Spirit of Truth instructs you. The Spirit of Truth cannot speak in error or lie.

Errors and lies are closely knit brethren and they are the products of the father of all lies and the Spirit of error. The Truth is that Paul was a convert. Before his conversion, Paul persecuted the believers of the Master Yahshua Messiah and partook in the murder of Stephen, the first martyr of the Faith. Paul's conversion happened on his way to Damascus to commit further atrocities against the believers of Yahshua Messiah in that city. He had an encounter with the Master along the way.

After the encounter, he was supposed to go and humble himself before the Apostles of the Master and learn from them the rudiments of the Faith as delivered to them by the Master. However, he didn't do so; rather, he relied on his training as a lawyer and as a student of the scriptures in the sect of the Pharisees. This is the cause of the errors of Paul which I intend to outline herein. These errors of Paul have since been the bane of Christians who follow Paul's understanding of the Faith, without recourse to the Master Yahshua Messiah and His original appointed Apostles.

Paul himself testified in his letter to the congregation in Galatia in Galatians 1:15-17:

*"But when it pleased Yahweh, who separated me from my mother's womb, and called me by his grace, To reveal his Son in me, that I might*

*preach him among the heathen; immediately I conferred not with flesh and blood: Neither went I up to Jerusalem to them which were apostles before me; but I went into Arabia, and returned again unto Damascus".*

A good look at Paul's work from his letters makes it clear that he was an evangelist and a prophet of Yahshua Messiah. There was no way or means by which he could have been an Apostle. He probably did not understand this fact or became conceited as evidenced in some of his writings.

A believer should know that in all the scriptures contained in the Bible, there is only one perfect character and that is the Master Yahshua of Nazareth — the Messiah himself. Any other person is a man born of flesh and prone to errors and failings, even when they are chosen and appointed by the Almighty. Paul is no exception.

Critical observation indicates that the errors of Paul are the bane of Christianity. Yes, Paul was converted by the Master, just as Jeroboam the Son of Nebat was chosen by the Almighty Yahweh Elohim of Israel to be the King of Ephraim, the Northern Kingdom of Israel. However, Jeroboam's error in judgment became the bane of that kingdom till the northern kingdom of Ephraim was cast out of the promised land and they became the lost tribes of Israel.

Apart from Jeroboam the son of Nebat, there are other instances of many who were chosen but committed terrible errors. We, however, cannot talk about them all or we will deviate completely from our focus. We have instances of people like Saul the son of Kish, Jehu the son of Nimshi, Solomon the son of King David, Aaron the priest, Gideon the judge, Eli the priest, Samson the judge, and so on. Our focus is, however, on Paul because of the effect his work and writings have on Christianity to this day.

Meanwhile, there are several errors in Christianity that did not arise from Paul. Many of them are due to the translation of the Bible from the original language. Several characters in the Old Covenant or Old Testament Scriptures are referenced in the New Covenant Scriptures. It is very disheartening to see that the names of such characters were clearly corrupted or changed since the transliteration of the names in the Old Covenant Scriptures is different from the transliteration of the same names in the New Covenant Scriptures. This ought not to be so irrespective of the source language. The fact remains that the present language is the same which is the English language for both the old and new covenant scriptures.

In the King James Version of the Bible in the Gospel of Matthew 3:3, we have the name of Prophet Isaiah changed to Esaias and the same error is repeated in several parts of the New Covenant Gospel scriptures. In Matthew 11:14 and other parts of the book, we have the name of Prophet Elijah changed to Elias. In Matthew 2:17, the name of Prophet Jeremiah was changed to Jeremy. In Matthew 24:37, the name Noah was changed to Noe, and so on. These are Old Covenant Scriptures characters whose names are spelt differently in the same English Bible and the translators and compilers could not notice the discrepancies.

This is apart from all the Jewish names of all the Jewish characters in the New Covenant Scriptures that were totally altered and changed thereby undermining the integrity of the information upon which the salvation of the human race is founded. These acts are offences of plagiarism and assault on the names and characters of the Scriptures. These offences were perpetrated in the Dark Ages and Yahshua Messiah spoke about them in the Gospel according to Matthew 11:12; ***"And from the days of John the Baptist until now the kingdom of heaven suffereth violence, and the violent take it by force"***.

It is bad enough that these alterations and changes were effected on the names of mere men. However, to go overboard to effect changes on the names of Yahweh Elohim the Almighty and of His only Begotten Son Yahshua Messiah is nothing short of a cosmic and spiritual crime. Only at the return and appearance of the Son of Yahweh will the pseudo-church understand the magnitude of the offence against uninformed believers who will be disappointed for building their Faith and making their sacrifices on a foundation of a false name, false identity and false doctrines.

# Chapter 2
# OPERATING THE SCRIPTURES

# OPERATING THE SCRIPTURES

Before we delve into some of the errors of Paul, we must establish an understanding of how to use the Scriptures which Paul himself wrote to a fellow he converted to the Faith — Timothy. In 2 Timothy 2:15, Paul says, ***"Study to shew thyself approved unto Yahweh, a workman that needeth not to be ashamed, rightly dividing the word of truth"***.

Although Paul had his errors, he was not always wrong or in error. If we indeed give the diligence to present ourselves approved by the Almighty Yahweh Elohim as workmen who do not need to be ashamed but properly handling the Word of Truth, then we will know how to properly divide and handle the scriptures without doing a disservice to the Spirit of the Scriptures, i.e. the Spirit of Truth.

As mentioned already, it is common knowledge that the Bible is divided into two parts: the Old Testament and the New Testament. Meanwhile, the word "Testament" is not proper since it doesn't connote the essence of the scriptures. In fact, the word 'Testament' is not mentioned even once in all of the so-called "Old Testament" scriptures. The right word or name, therefore, ought to be "Covenant". Again, we see a deliberately infused error in the scriptures. The Bible should have been rightly divided into the Old Covenant Scriptures and the New Covenant Scriptures because the relationship with Yahweh the Elohim of Israel is a Covenant to make Him Lord and Deity over whoever enters into the covenant with Him.

However, as a prophet of Yahshua Messiah myself, I observe by spiritual revelation that a better and more precise way to divide the Scriptures would be into three parts: 1. **The Law,** 2. **The Prophets** and 3. **The Gospel.**

If we follow this method of dividing the Scriptures, we will realize with clarity that Paul's letters are not part of the Scriptures because he did not walk with the Messiah physically. Hence, without any physical experience with Yahshua Messiah, Paul is not in a position to pen down any information (about his gospel of Yahshua Messiah) that is in any way equivalent to that of those who witnessed the physical existence of Yahshua Messiah, i.e the writers of the four available Gospels contained in the Bible.

Paul will, therefore, stand as probably the most prominent among the category of believers whom Yahshua Messiah blessed in the Gospel account of John 20:29: ***"Yahshua saith unto him, "Thomas, because thou hast seen me, thou hast believed: blessed are they that have not seen, and yet have believed".***

Although Paul wrote that he was the last to see Yahshua Messiah, what he saw of Yahshua Messiah was a vision and not the physical appearance of and interaction with Yahshua Messiah as the original Apostles and disciples of Yahshua Messiah experienced.

With this division of the Scriptures into the Law, the Prophets and the Gospel, we discover that Paul in all his writings wrote from his understanding of the Spirit along with the Scriptures of the Law and the Prophets. Obviously, he did not write from an actual memory of a physical walk and experience with the Master. The Master Yahshua attests to this very deduction in John.14:26; ***"But the Counselor, the Holy Spirit, whom the Father will send in my name, he will teach you all things, and will remind you of all that I said to you".***

Paul did not know what the Master taught and said to His Apostles and disciples. Therefore, he should have humbled himself to be schooled by the Apostles, which he confirmed that he didn't do especially as there were no written Gospels by the Apostles in the days of Paul as we have readily in the Bible today.

With this understanding, we can appreciate why there could have been doctrinal errors in Paul's writings concerning the Master's Word and teachings, not forgetting the word of the Master Yahshua Messiah in the Gospel according to John 8:31; ***"If ye continue in my word, then are ye my disciples indeed;"***

The Gospels provide us with the Word of the Master Yahshua Messiah to enable our discipleship. The recording of the Gospels is the most important reason why the Master Yahshua Messiah elected the twelve Apostles as His foundational witnesses.

# SPIRIT

When we talk about Elohim or God, we talk about Yahweh. In John 4:24, Yahshua Messiah our Master and teacher taught us that ***"Elohim is Spirit: and they that worship him must worship him in spirit and in truth."***

## WHAT IS A SPIRIT?

According to the English dictionary, a spirit is an animating or vital 'principle' held to give life to physical organisms. Also, the spirit is the activating or essential 'principle' influencing a person.

In dealing with a Spirit, we deal with principles. A principle is a comprehensive and fundamental law, assumption or doctrine. For example, the Master Yahshua Messiah told us about the Holy Spirit in the Gospel according to Apostle John 15:26; ***"When the Advocate comes, whom I will send to you from the Father —the Spirit of Truth who goes out from the Father —he will testify about me.***

The principle of the Holy Spirit, therefore, is Truth. Hence, the Holy Spirit cannot be part of a lie or an error. To receive the Spirit of Yahweh is to receive the principle of Yahweh, which is the law of Yahweh.

When reading the Scriptures in respect of the Holy Spirit, I prefer the translation 'Advocate' and 'Counselor' over 'Comforter', because the Holy Spirit comes to reveal truths about the Master to us as disciples; He reminds us of His teachings. These are not the roles of a comforter.

# TESTING OF EVERY SPIRIT

As believers, we must understand the concept of spirits and the fact that a spirit is the essential animating principle that gives life to a living organism. Therefore, there is a spirit behind every organism and every operation. The spirit or principle that animates aquatic organisms is different from the spirit or principle of terrestrial organisms. The spirit or principle of democracy is different from the principle or spirit of monarchy. With this understanding, we should delve into the advice and warning of the Apostle John to the church in 1 John 4:1; ***"Beloved, believe not every spirit, but try the spirits whether they are of Yahweh: because many false prophets are gone out into the world."***

John is one of the twelve Apostles genuinely appointed by Yahshua Messiah. John is the Apostle who saw the Yahshua 'that was' (which is Yahshua of Nazareth before His crucifixion), the Yahshua Messiah "that is" after His resurrection and the Yahshua that is "to come" after his ascension into heaven to be at the right hand of the throne of the Father Yahweh. Therefore, the words and messages of John concerning the understanding of the Faith of Yahshua Messiah are profound and deep. More importantly, the Apostle John was one of the "top three" most intimate Apostles of the Master who witnessed the transfiguration of our Master Yahshua Messiah that was.

John, in his writing in 1 John 4:1, is saying that many spirits have entered into the world to operate according to their essential principles. The spirits that John referred to are specific; they are different and contrary to the Spirit of Yahweh. These contrary Spirits of Falsehood operating in false prophets are also competing with the Spirit of Yahweh for the souls of men.

The Spirit of Obedience is different from the Spirit of Disobedience. Both spirits can be determined and differentiated by their essential principles. A spirit that obeys the commandment of Yahweh like remembering the Sabbaths of Yahweh and hallowing them is a Spirit of Obedience. A Spirit that undermines and disregards the Sabbaths of Yahweh and is less perturbed about keeping them holy is a Spirit of Disobedience.

Regardless of the kind of sacrifices, offerings and thanksgiving offered with the spirit of disobedience, it remains the spirit of disobedience by its essential principles. For this reason, the Scriptures records in 1Samuel 15:22-23;

***"And Samuel said, Hath Yahweh as great delight in burnt offerings and sacrifices, as in obeying the voice of Yahweh? Behold, to obey is better than sacrifice, and to hearken than the fat of rams. For rebellion is as the sin of witchcraft, and stubbornness is as iniquity and idolatry......"***

This assessment of the underlying principle is the fundamental way to test a spirit and determine its nature and essence. There are many spirits. Apart from the countless spirits of nature, there is the Spirit of Truth and there is the Spirit of Error. There is the Spirit of Witchcraft, which is in tandem with the Spirit of Rebellion. There are lying spirits, familiar spirits, unclean spirits and all sorts of spirits.

We must understand and know which spirits pertain to and operate with the Spirit of Yahweh and which spirits are not of Yahweh. The vital principles behind each spirit determine what kind the spirit is.

Paul mentioned a gift of discerning spirits in his first letter to the congregation in Corinth — 1Corinthians 12:10; ***"To another the working of miracles; to another prophecy; to another "discerning of spirits"; to another divers kinds of tongues; to another the interpretation of tongues:***

However, what the Apostle John is talking about is not the gift of discerning or discernment of spirits but the determining of spirits by using the word of Yahweh as a litmus test. To explain further, one may encounter someone operating with the spirit of prophecy or peeping into spiritual realms to gather intelligence, which is divination. That someone has this kind of spirit does not mean the person is operating with the Spirit of Yahweh.

By testing the operation of such spirit with the word of Yahweh, we can determine if the spirit is of Yahweh or contrary to the Spirit of Yahweh. So also, we can test any office, minister, doctrine, sermon, teaching or point with the word of Yahweh to determine if the fundamental spirit operating is the Spirit of Truth or the Spirit of error. This is what it means to test every spirit.

## THE SPIRIT OF ERROR

The term 'error' comes from the verb 'err'. To err is to make a mistake, to violate an accepted standard of conduct.

A mistake is to blunder in choice. To make mistakes is to misunderstand and misinterpret the meaning or intention of a subject, to make a wrong judgment, a wrong action or a wrong statement proceeding from faulty judgment, inadequate knowledge or inattention.

An error is an act or condition of ignorant or imprudent deviation from a code of behaviour; an act involving an unintentional deviation from 'truth' or 'accuracy'. An error is also an act that, through ignorance, deficiency, or accident, departs from or fails to achieve what should be achieved.

In religious practices, the quality or state of erring or committing an error is any instance of false belief.

In mathematical parlance, an error is the difference between an observed or calculated value and a true value. An error is also a deficiency or imperfection in structure or function.

These definitions presented as the vital principle of any operation would determine the operation to be a function of the Spirit of Error. This spirit of error can function in any person, action, doctrine, and teaching, to name a few. When the spirit of error functions in any operation, it makes the operation false. Where teachings contain errors, the word of Yahweh, through the Prophet Isaiah, speaks thus — Isaiah 32:6;

*"For the fool will speak folly, and his heart will work iniquity, to practice profanity, and to utter error against Yahweh, To make empty the soul of the hungry, and to cause the drink of the thirsty to fail"*.

The Spirit of Error operates in believers and adherents of the faith. The scriptures clarify that the leadership and leaders of the faith are the cause of this situation. We see this in Isaiah 9:16; *"For the leaders of this people cause them to err; and they that are led of them are destroyed..."*

The error that led to the destruction and dispersion of the Northern Kingdom of Israel came from the first king of Israel chosen by Yahweh. That king was Jeroboam the Son of Nebat, and we find a record of this in the Scriptures of 1Kings 14:15-16;

*"For Yahweh shall smite Israel, as a reed is shaken in the water, and he shall root up Israel out of this good land, which he gave to their fathers, and shall scatter them beyond the river, because they have made their groves, provoking Yahweh to anger. And he shall give Israel up because of the sins of Jeroboam, who did sin, and who made Israel to sin".*

Also, on another occasion, during the journey of the Israelites to the Promised Land of Canaan, the error of the Golden Calf was initiated by Aaron the High Priest who happened to be the brother of Moses. We find some details of this in the Scriptures of Exodus 32:3-6;

*"And all the people brake off the golden earrings which were in their ears, and brought them unto Aaron. And he received them at their hand, and fashioned it with a graving tool, after he had made it a molten calf: and they said, These be thy Elohim, O Israel, which brought thee up out of the land of Egypt. And when Aaron saw it, he built an altar before it; and Aaron made proclamation, and said, Tomorrow is a feast to Yahweh. And they rose up early on the morrow, and offered burnt offerings, and brought peace offerings; and the people sat down to eat and to drink, and rose up to play".*

We see how this grave error was delivered to the people by their leader.

Gideon the Judge, a mighty man of valour chosen by Yahweh to be a leader, also made an ephod from the gold collection when Yahweh gave him victory over the Midianites and the Amalekites. Over time, the children of Israel started worshipping the ephod and this became a snare and an entanglement for the house of Gideon. We find this account in the Scriptures of Judges 8:25-27;

*"And they answered, We will willingly give them. And they spread a garment, and did cast therein every man the earrings of his prey. And the weight of the golden earrings that he requested was a thousand and seven hundred shekels of gold; beside ornaments, and collars, and purple raiment that was on the kings of Midian, and beside the chains that were about their camels necks. And Gideon made an ephod thereof, and put it in his city, even in Ophrah: and all Israel went thither a whoring after it: which thing became a snare unto Gideon, and to his house".*

From these accounts carefully recorded in the Scriptures, a sincere seeker and believer of the Truth will see that just because a man is chosen by Yahweh does not mean he is no longer human or susceptible to error. Therefore, as a believer you must test what you hear and see at any point in time to determine the spirit in operation.

We have established already that the Spirit of Error is a function of misconception, misunderstanding, and misinterpretation of the Scriptures. Sometimes, it is fuelled by the spirit of greed, covetousness, lust for power and control of subjects and may be accompanied by the spirits of rebellion and stubbornness. Every misunderstanding, misconception and misinterpretation of the Scripture is the work and operation of the Spirit of Error. In Mark 12:24, Yahshua Messiah, the perfect Master, addressed the Sadducees, a leading religious sect among the Jews then, thus: *"And Yahshua answering said unto them, Do ye not therefore err, because ye know not the scriptures, neither the power of Yahweh?*

In operating with the Scriptures, the power of Yahweh is demonstrated by delivering the very truth on any matter. Contrarily, to stand in error is to be under the influence of a power apart and separate from that of the power of Yahweh and contrary to the truth irrespective of persons involved or location. Error is error and error is always the corruption of the truth. It is designed and infused into doctrines by the devil who is the enemy of the truth.

We, therefore, can confidently say that anyone, irrespective of position or age, who we observe to be in error, is under the influence of the enemy. The Spirit of Error is a twin brother of the Spirit of Lies and Falsehood. To point out an error is crucial to our faith as believers in the Kingdom of Heaven and the Kingship of Yahshua Messiah.

This is clearly outlined in the letter of James (the brother of our Messiah) to the church in James 5:19-20;

*"Brethren, if any of you do err from the truth, and one convert him; Let him know, that he which converteth the sinner from the error of his way shall save a soul from death, and shall hide a multitude of sins".*

There is a Spirit of Error operating among professed believers, and I dare say much of it originated from the writings of Paul the evangelist. We must be aware of it in order to deal with it. We ought to do so as we contend for the Kingdom and the Word of Yahweh.

## THE HOLY SPIRIT

We must consciously and continually note that there are many different spirits. After all, the Advocate (sometimes translated as Helper or Comforter) which we are to receive as believers after activating our rebirth in Yahshua Messiah is also a Spirit.

Yahweh told us a lot about the Messiah in the prophecies recorded by His prophets and holy men. The Messiah was to come as a man; hence, there would always have been many men who would dare to falsely claim to be the expected or promised Messiah. Yahshua the Messiah in truth and verity talked about these categories of people in the Gospel according to John in John 10:8; *"All that ever came before me are thieves and robbers: but the sheep did not hear them".*

Yahshua is saying that anyone anywhere, and at any time, who claimed to be the Messiah, apart from Himself, was a very cosmic and spiritual criminal.

Just as there are criminal elements among men falsely claiming to be the promised Messiah, there are also **lying spirits, familiar spirits, and spirits of error appearing to people and claiming to be the very Holy Spirit** promised by the Messiah and sent to the first set of believers to be the founding members of the Church of Yahshua Messiah.

Spirits are invisible but are discernable (visible) in the spiritual realm. However, the Holy Spirit is invisible in both the spiritual and physical realms. We certainly read of an apparition of a dove descending upon Yahshua Messiah during his immersion at the Jordan River by the Prophet John as recorded in the Gospel according to John in John 1:32; *"And John bare record, saying, I saw the Spirit descending from heaven like a dove, and it abode upon him"*.

This apparition is a deliberate operation by the power of Yahweh for the people witnessing the event to understand that there is a divine presence among them. Another apparition was seen during the Holy Spirit fire immersion of the founding members of the church as recorded in Acts 2:1-4;

*"And when the day of Pentecost was fully come, they were all with one accord in one place. And suddenly there came a sound from heaven as of a rushing mighty wind, and it filled the entire house where they were sitting. And there appeared unto them cloven tongues like as of fire, and it sat upon each of them. And they were all filled with the Holy Spirit, and began to speak with other tongues, as the Spirit gave them utterance"*

These are deliberate apparitions. The Holy Spirit remains invisible in the physical and spiritual realms, whereas other spirits are visible in their shapes and forms in the spiritual realm. The invisibility of the Holy Spirit in both the physical and spiritual realms is the reason why there are no divinations, enchantments or sorcery that is potent against the Holy Spirit and those operating in and with the Holy Spirit.

# HOW DO YOU KNOW YOU ARE OPERATING IN AND WITH THE HOLY SPIRIT?

The first and most important aspect of the Holy Spirit is 'Truth' — starting with Scriptural and Spiritual Truths. The essence and vital principle of the Holy Spirit being the Truth is highlighted by the Master Yahshua Messiah in the Gospel according to Apostle John in John 14:16-17;

*"And I will pray the Father, and he shall give you another Counselor, that he may abide with you forever; Even the Spirit of truth; whom the world cannot receive, because it seeth him not, neither knoweth him: but ye know him; for he dwelleth with you, and shall be in you".*

The Master repeats this position in the Gospel of Apostle John in John15:26-27;

*"But when the Counselor is come, whom I will send unto you from the Father, even the Spirit of truth, which proceedeth from the Father, he shall testify of me: And ye also shall bear witness, because ye have been with me from the beginning".*

It is, therefore, a certain sign and confirmable proof that one is operating with and in the Holy Spirit every time one is speaking and demonstrating the Truth with the Scriptures, especially concerning Yahshua Messiah and His Kingship over the Kingdom of Heaven and of Yahweh.

The second sign and proof that a person is operating with and in the Holy Spirit is that the spirit must come in the name of Yahshua Messiah. The name of Yahshua Messiah is so vital and sacred that it should never have been translated or interpolated. Of course, no person will accept that their names be unduly translated or interpolated just because there is a transfer of information from one language to another. I mean a name can always be transliterated from one alphabetic system to another, but to translate or interpolate a person's name due to a change of language or alphabetic system is an unacceptable and generally illegal act.

The transliteration of the Messiah's earthly name is Yahoshua contracted to Yahshua. Therefore and to reiterate, the name Jesus is simply an unacceptable interpolation, and the error has been accepted and corrected in the Restored Name King James Version (RNKJV) by some publishers of the King James Version of the Bible being the most widespread and widely read version.

The spirit that will manifest in the name "Jesus Christ' is different from the spirit that will manifest in the name "Yahshua Messiah" because these are two different names literally and spiritually. Different names control different spirits just as it is with people; different people bear and answer to different names. It is the same with organizations and nations. The Master asserts in the Gospel according to Apostle John in John 14:14; *"If ye shall ask any thing in MY NAME, I will do it"*. The emphasis is on 'in my name", which is different from **"in any name you choose to call me"**.

The third sign and proof of the Holy Spirit is the Word and commandments of Yahweh the Elohim of Israel and Yahshua Messiah. The Master, in the Gospel according to Apostle John in John 14:21 said;

*"He that hath my commandments, and keepeth them, he it is that loveth me: and he that loveth me shall be loved of my Father, and I will love him, and will manifest myself to him"*.

If a person is disobedient to the commandments and ordinances of Yahweh Elohim and Yahshua Messiah as contained in the Scriptures of the Bible, such a person cannot be operating with the Spirit of Yahweh or of Yahshua Messiah, which is the Spirit of Truth (being the Holy Spirit). The Spirit of Truth makes us holy because the Spirit of Truth is the Holy Spirit. Without Truth, all activities we do for Yahweh are unacceptable. Hence, Yahshua Messiah, in John 14:6, affirmed that He is the Truth, the Way and the Life — "Yahshua saith unto him, *I am the way, the truth, and the life: no man cometh unto the Father, but by me"*.

# CONTENDING FOR THE FAITH

Judah, who wrote the letter titled Jude to the Church, was not one of the twelve Apostles appointed by the Master Yahshua Messiah; however, he was a biological brother of Yahshua Messiah maternally and was mentioned in the Gospel according to Matthew in Matthew 13:54-55;

*"And when he was come into his own country, he taught them in their synagogue, insomuch that they were astonished, and said, Whence hath this man this wisdom, and these mighty works? Is not this the carpenters son? is not his mother called Mary? and his brethren, James, and Joses, and Simon, and Judah?*

And in his letter, Judah the brother of our Savior wrote in Jude 1:3-4;

*"Beloved, when I gave all diligence to write unto you of the common salvation, it was needful for me to write unto you, and exhort you that ye should earnestly contend for the faith which was once delivered unto the saints. For there are certain men crept in unawares, who were before of old ordained to this condemnation, wicked men, turning the grace of our Elohim into lasciviousness, and denying the only Master Elohim, and our Master Yahshua the Messiah"*.

He talked about a **"common salvation"** which is shared by believers. Hence, all believers are supposed to share the same salvation. And regarding that common salvation, he exhorts that every believer should contend for the faith of salvation. To contend is to strive, to vie in a contest, to struggle in debate by arguments, to maintain and assert a position or a principle.

In Luke 13:24, the Master Yahshua Messiah also told his followers and believers to strive for entry at the strait and difficult gate: *"Strive to enter in at the strait gate: for many, I say unto you, will seek to enter in, and shall not be able"*.

The strait gate is the lawful and legitimate entry into the sheepfold. Paul attests to this when he wrote to Timothy in 2 Timothy 2:5; *"And if a man also strive for masteries, yet is he not crowned, except he strive lawfully"*.

This position is correct. An athlete does not receive the medal or victor's crown except by competing according to the rules and regulations of the sport.

Therefore, we have to contend and strive lawfully for the Faith delivered only once and for all to the saints. Faith is not just mere belief. No matter how strong the belief is, it is merely a belief and not Faith. Rather, Faith is a mixture of Belief with, most importantly, understanding, knowledge and wisdom. Belief without understanding and knowledge is blind. Such belief is comparable to that of the foolish virgins mentioned in the Parable of Ten Virgins taught by the Master Yahshua Messiah.

As a serious believer, one must know and understand what exactly one believes. It, therefore, becomes necessary to scrutinize the information regarding the belief. As believers, we ought to contend and strive for the original information that was delivered to the original Apostles. We are not meant to accept adulterations or fabrications.

Our Common Salvation by the One and only Saviour is deliverance from the following;

1. Ignorance,

2. Illusion,

3. The coming judgment and destruction,

4. The power and effective control of sin,

5. Present difficulties of persecution

When we are ignorant, we are in darkness. Also, when we believe in an illusion, we are in darkness as well. When we are under the control and power of sin, we are in darkness still. Yahshua Messiah admonishes his followers in the Gospel according to Apostle John in John 8:12; *"Yahshua spake again*

***unto them, saying, I am the light of the world: he that followeth me shall not walk in darkness, but shall have the light of life".***

Believers must perform frequent checks on themselves to know if they are following Yahshua Messiah or following their preferred pastor or denomination. A believer must spend quality time to know Yahshua Messiah and understand the Faith more deeply in the Truth. A man's level of understanding determines who he is in the Kingdom, not how long he has been professing the Faith and not how much money he has or the material assets he gathers by greed and subtle manipulation of the gullible and uninformed believers.

The problem with organized religion today is the complex between the leaders and the followers. The leaders sense and discover by subtle means what the followers desire and manipulate them by false prophesyings and long prayers of dissimulation.

Meanwhile, we must never forget that all the children of Israel who left Egypt went through the Red Sea on dry ground, and were under the pillar of cloud by day. They were all led by Moses the servant of Yahweh and ate Manna, which was a spiritual food. They drank the miraculous water that came out of a rock. However, with most of them, Yahweh was not pleased. Hence, many of them perished in the wilderness, never making it to the Promised Land.

All the details in the Scriptures were recorded with obvious sincerity and kept for us lest we proceed blindly in the Faith of Salvation with ignorance and mere belief. By obtaining knowledge and understanding, we ought to contend for the Faith delivered once and for all by the Master Yahshua Messiah to his original Apostles.

# Chapter 3
# DOCTRINAL ERRORS OF PAUL

# SOME OF PAUL'S DOCTRINAL ERRORS

We are examining the list of Paul's doctrinal errors to shake up and wake up the sleeping believers. The goal is to cause a genuine revival of Truth within the church and among believers of Yahshua Messiah. As we begin this revival of Truth, we ought to do it with the understanding from Ecclesiastes10:1; *"Dead flies cause the ointment of the apothecary to send forth a stinking savour: so doth a little folly him that is in reputation for wisdom and honour"*.

We should recall also Galatians 5:9; *"A little leaven leaveneth the whole lump"*.

Therefore, we are picking out the doctrinal errors to expel the dead flies from the ointment of doctrines and remove the leaven from the dough of our Faith so that we may become the unleavened bread that accompanies our Passover which is the person of Yahshua our Messiah.

Whenever we talk about the Kingdom of Heaven or the Kingdom of Yahweh, we are talking about and proclaiming the kingship and reign of Yahshua of Nazareth the Messiah.

Paul was no doubt a great and enthusiastic evangelist who was eager to spread the good news of the Kingdom of Yahweh and the Kingship of Yahshua Messiah, considering the level of grace and mercy he received from the Master Yahshua Messiah after he persecuted the believers and followers of Yahshua Messiah. However, he had his shortcomings in that he did not receive direct tutelage and mentorship from the Master Yahshua Messiah, and he did not humble himself under any of the genuine Apostles to learn from them and to know what they had heard and learnt from the Master Yahshua Messiah.

It is not enough to believe and confess that Yahshua Messiah is your Lord and Saviour. Yahshua Messiah made it clear in the Gospel according to Matthew in Matthew 7:21; *"Not every one that saith unto me, Rabbi, Rabbi, shall enter into the kingdom of heaven; but he that doeth the will of my Father which is in heaven"*.

Interestingly, Paul teaches something contrary to the Master's Word. Hence, what Paul wrote in his letter to the congregation in Rome in Romans10:9 should be considered an error: *"That if thou shalt confess with thy mouth that Yahshua is the Messiah, and shalt believe in thine heart that Yahweh hath raised him from the dead, thou shalt be saved"*.

The Master clearly says that it is not enough to believe and confess; something extra must be done to ascertain one's salvation and admission into the Kingdom of Heaven. That extra thing has to do with the **will** and **expectations** of the **Father** of our Master Yahshua Messiah.

Paul himself was learned as a Pharisee by discipline. However, from the Gospels, we understand that the teachings of the Pharisees were different from the teachings of Yahshua Messiah in many ways and aspects. I came to the point of discussing this important topic because I received these teachings and understanding of the Word of the Master Yahshua Messiah by revelations from the Father through the Holy Spirit of Yahweh.

Talking about spirits, there are many spirits as we have seen already in this book as well as in several parts of the Holy Scriptures. Meanwhile, it is quite possible for many spirits can possess an individual at the same time. To establish this assertion, let us consider Mary of Magdala called Mary Magdalene in the Gospel according to Mark 16:9; *"Now when Yahshua was risen early the first day of the week, he appeared first to Mary Magdalene, out of whom he had cast seven devils"*.

Here, we read and understand that there were seven (7) devils or evil spirits residing in the woman, possessing and oppressing her at the same time.

Also, let's examine the case of the Lunatic of Gadarenes in the Gospel according to Mark in Mark 5:7-9;

*"And cried with a loud voice, and said, What have I to do with thee, Yahshua, thou Son of the most high Elohim? I adjure thee by Elohim, that thou torment me not. For he said unto him, Come out of the man, thou*

*unclean spirit. And he asked him, what is thy name? And he answered, saying, my name is Legion: for we are many.*

Here, we understand that a legion of devils and unclean spirits were dwelling in this man. By the way, a legion comprises a minimum of five thousand (5,000) soldiers.

It is also established from the Scriptures that there are unclean spirits, familiar spirits, witchcraft spirits and so on. Also, there are lying spirits and spirits of error. That Yahweh appoints a person does not mean that such a person will not be confronted by contrary spirits. We can learn this fact from the story of Adam, Moses, Aaron, Saul, David, Jeroboam, and Solomon. Even the Master Yahshua Messiah was confronted by the devil in temptation.

Therefore, anyone in the Kingdom operation of Yahweh Elohim can fall into errors orchestrated by contrary spirits at any point in time. That is one of the points that make Yahshua our Messiah so special and important as we see in the prophecy of the Prophet Isaiah in Isaiah 11:1-5;

*"And there shall come forth a rod out of the stem of Jesse, and a Branch shall grow out of his roots: And the spirit of Yahweh shall rest upon him, the spirit of wisdom and understanding, the spirit of counsel and might, the spirit of knowledge and of the fear of Yahweh; And shall make him of quick understanding in the fear of Yahweh: and he shall not judge after the sight of his eyes, neither reprove after the hearing of his ears: But with righteousness shall he judge the poor, and reprove with equity for the meek of the earth: and he shall smite the earth with the rod of his mouth, and with the breath of his lips shall he slay the wicked. And righteousness shall be the girdle of his loins, and faithfulness the girdle of his reins".*

# THE ERRORS

The first error of Paul I will point out is in his first letter to the congregation in Corinth in 1Corinthians 4:15;

*'For though ye have ten thousand instructors in the Messiah, yet have ye not many 'fathers': for in the Messiah Yahshua I have begotten you through the evangel".*

This statement may look flawless but it is in direct disobedience to the Master's command in the Gospel of Matthew in Matthew 23:8-10;

*"But be not ye called Rabbi: for one is your Rabbi, even the Messiah; and all ye are brethren. And call no man your father upon the earth: for one is your Father, which is in heaven. Neither be ye called masters: for one is your master, even the Messiah."*

So, Paul started this trend of calling himself a father to other believers and that has been imitated by Christians till this very day against the command and instruction of the Saviour, Master and Messiah Yahshua of Nazareth.

Paul asserts this position again in his first letter to Timothy in 1 Timothy 1:2; *'Unto Timothy, my own son in the faith: Grace, mercy, and peace, from Yahweh our Father and Yahshua the Messiah our Master."*

Designating Timothy as his son in the Faith was in contrast with the teachings of the Master Yahshua Messiah and, therefore, it is an error with a spirit of disobedience to the Master and Savior that has been absorbed and adopted by Christians to this day.

**THE LAW IS A TEACHER.**

Another error of Paul is to state that the Law is a teacher, whereas the Law of Yahweh is not a teacher. Yahshua Messiah is the only perfect standard and that is why He is the only begotten SON of Yahweh and the only Master teacher for a true believer.

Let's consider what Paul wrote to the congregation in Galatia in Galatians 3:24-25;

*"Wherefore the law was our schoolmaster to bring us unto the Messiah, that we might be justified by faith. But after that faith is come, we are no longer under a schoolmaster".*

This is an erroneous statement by which Paul continues to undermine the Law of Yahweh. After all, the Master taught in Matthew.5:17-18;

*"Think not that I am come to destroy the law, or the prophets: I am not come to destroy, but to fulfill. For verily I say unto you, till heaven and earth pass, one jot or one tittle shall in no wise pass from the law, till all be fulfilled".*

As a Pharisee and astute student of the Law, Paul did not come to Yahshua by the Law; rather, his enthusiasm about the Law made him a persecutor of Yahshua Messiah's disciples as recorded in the Acts of the Apostles — Acts.22:1-10;

*"Men, brethren, and fathers, hear ye my defence which I make now unto you. (And when they heard that he spake in the Hebrew tongue to them, they kept the more silence: and he saith,) I am verily a man which am a Jew, born in Tarsus, a city in Cilicia, yet brought up in this city at the feet of Gamaliel, and taught according to the perfect manner of the law of the fathers, and was zealous toward Elohim, as ye all are this day. And I persecuted this way unto the death, binding and delivering into prisons both men and women. As also the high priest doth bear me witness, and all the estate of the elders: from whom also I received letters unto the brethren, and went to Damascus, to bring them which were there bound unto Jerusalem, for to be punished. And it came to pass, that, as I made my journey, and was come nigh unto Damascus about noon, suddenly there shone from heaven a great light round about me. And I fell unto the ground, and heard a voice saying unto me, Saul, Saul, why persecutest thou me? And I answered, who art thou, Master? And he said unto me, I am Yahshua of Nazareth, whom thou persecutest. And they that were*

*with me saw indeed the light, and were afraid; but they heard not the voice of him that spake to me. And I said, what shall I do, master? And Yahshua said unto me, Arise, and go into Damascus; and there it shall be told thee of all things which are appointed for thee to do".*

So, even though Saul (later known as Paul) was called by Yahshua Messiah, he had entered into a doctrinal error at this point. Here is what Yahshua Messiah the Master and teacher taught us as disciples in the gospel according to John in John 6:44-46;

*"No man can come to me, except the Father which hath sent me draw him: and I will raise him up at the last day. It is written in the prophets, And they shall be all taught of Yahweh. Every man therefore that hath heard, and hath learned of the Father, cometh unto me..."*

This position is confirmed also in the prophecy of Isaiah in Isaiah 54:13; *"All your children shall be taught of Yahweh; and great shall be the peace of your children."*

We see it also in the prophecy of Jeremiah in Jeremiah 31:31-34;

*"Behold, the days come, saith Yahweh, that I will make a 'new covenant' with the house of Israel, and with the house of Judah: Not according to the covenant that I made with their fathers in the day that I took them by the hand to bring them out of the land of Egypt; which my covenant they brake, although I was an husband unto them, saith Yahweh: But this shall be the covenant that I will make with the house of Israel; After those days, saith Yahweh, I will put my law in their inward parts, and write it in their hearts; and will be their Elohim, and they shall be my people. And they shall teach no more every man his neighbor and every man his brother, saying, Know Yahweh: for they shall all know me, from the least of them unto the greatest of them, saith Yahweh; for I will forgive their iniquity, and I will remember their sin no more".*

This New Covenant is what the Christians call the New Testament, which was what the Master was referring to when He spoke to His Apostles in Matthew 26:28; *"for this is my blood of the new covenant, which is poured out for many for the remission of sins."*

From the Prophecy of Jeremiah, we see that the Law of Yahweh will be taught, put and inscribed in the hearts of true believers by Yahweh Himself and so therefore the Law is not the teacher or schoolmaster by itself as propounded by Paul.


## REDEEMED FROM UNDER THE LAW

Paul wrote to the congregation in Galatia in Galatians4:1-5;

*"Now I say, That the heir, as long as he is a child, differeth nothing from a servant, though he be master of all; But is under tutors and governors until the time appointed of the father. Even so we, when we were children, were in bondage under the elements of the world: But when the fullness of the time was come, Yahweh sent forth his Son, made of a woman, made under the law, To redeem them that were under the law, that we might receive the adoption of sons".*

However, when we compare Paul's statement to the Galatians here with the commission and assignment he received from the Master, we notice another error and discrepancy;

Acts 26:16-18;

*"But rise, and stand upon thy feet: for I have appeared unto thee for this purpose, to make thee a minister and a witness both of these things which thou hast seen, and of those things in which I will appear unto thee; Delivering thee from the people, and from the Gentiles, unto whom now I send thee, To open their eyes, and to turn them from darkness to light, and from the power of Satan unto Yahweh, that they may receive forgiveness of sins, and inheritance among them which are sanctified by faith that is in me.*

Now, it is reasonable to ask, **was the Law of Yahweh the darkness and power of Satan from which the Gentiles or even the Jews were delivered, according to the instructions given by the Master Yahshua Messiah to Paul in his vision?** Certainly not! The Scriptures record in Proverbs 6:23;

*"For the commandment is a lamp; and the <u>Law is light;</u> and reproofs of instruction are the way of life:"*

And also Psalms 119:105; *"<u>Thy</u> word is a lamp unto my feet, and a <u>light</u> unto my path"*.

That we become Sons of Yahweh does not make us above the Law of Yahweh. "No one is above the Law" is a very common saying which is never refuted. Paul wrote to the Romans in Romans 8:19; *"For the earnest expectation of the creature waiteth for the manifestation of th<u>e sons of Yahweh</u>"*.

However, John records in his Gospel in John 1:12; *"But as many as received him, to them gave he power to become the <u>sons of Yahweh</u>, even to them that believe on his name"*:

And Yahweh says to His Sons in His word in Proverbs 3:1-4;

*"My son, <u>forget not my law;</u> but let <u>thine heart keep my commandments:</u> For length of days, and long life, and peace, shall they add to thee. Let not mercy and truth forsake thee: bind them about thy neck; write them upon the table of thine heart: So shalt thou find favour and good understanding in the sight of Elohim and man"*.

So, we see that there was this error of discarding the Law of Yahweh in the letter of Paul to the Galatian congregation. This error still plagues believers, especially Christians, today.

# PAUL'S TEACHING ON ABRAHAM

Paul wrote in his letter to the Roman congregation in Romans 4:3; *"For what saith the scripture? Abraham believed Yahweh, and it was counted unto him for righteousness"*.

This statement is indeed from the Scriptures of Genesis 15:6, but it is incomplete as basis of a doctrine for new converts and proselytes because a convert will not see and understand that to believe practically is to obey. Hence, Paul should have rather quoted Genesis 22:17-18;

*"That in blessing I will bless thee, and in multiplying I will multiply thy seed as the stars of the heaven, and as the sand which is upon the sea shore; and thy seed shall possess the gate of his enemies; And in thy seed shall all the nations of the earth be blessed; because thou hast OBEYED my voice.*

We see that the element of obedience is the substance of belief and not just confession. Also, Yahweh Elohim confirmed this position to Isaac the son of Abraham in Genesis 26:4-5;

*"And I will make thy seed to multiply as the stars of heaven, and will give unto thy seed all these countries; and in thy seed shall all the nations of the earth be blessed; Because that Abraham obeyed my voice, and kept my charge, my commandments, my statutes, and my laws."*

Here, in the Scriptures, Yahweh Elohim clarifies what Abraham OBEYED and what needs to be OBEYED by a genuine believer or convert.

# BETWEEN PAUL AND JAMES

Paul presents a doctrinal exegesis in his letter to the Roman congregation in Romans 4:1-5;

*"What shall we say then that Abraham our father, as pertaining to the flesh, hath found? For if Abraham were justified by works, he hath whereof to glory; but not before Yahweh. For what saith the scripture? Abraham believed Yahweh, and it was counted unto him for righteousness. Now to him that worketh is the reward not reckoned of grace, but of debt. But to him that worketh not, but believeth on him that justifieth the unrighteous, his faith is counted for righteousness.*

However, James a maternal brother of Yahshua Messiah, also handles the same doctrine differently in his letter to the church in James 2:19-26;

*"Thou believest that there is one Elohim; thou doest well: the devils also believe, and tremble. But wilt thou know, O vain man, that faith without works is dead? Was not Abraham our father justified by works, when he had offered Isaac his son upon the altar? Seest thou how faith wrought with his works, and by works was faith made perfect? And the scripture was fulfilled which saith, Abraham believed Yahweh, and it was imputed unto him for righteousness: and he was called the Friend of Yahweh. Ye see then how that by works a man is justified, and not by faith (belief) only. Likewise also was not Rahab the harlot justified by works, when she had received the messengers, and had sent them out another way? For as the body without the spirit is dead, so faith (actually mere belief) without works is dead also.*

Both positions of Paul and James cannot be correct at the same time; only one can be correct and true while the other remains incorrect, erroneous and false. So, based on our understanding as sincere believers who endeavour to serve Yahweh in truth and in spirit, we must ask ourselves in sincerity, who is correct between Paul and James?

Let us scrutinize the story of Abraham again. It begins in Genesis 12:1-4;

*"Now Yahweh had said unto Abram, Get thee out of thy country, and from thy kindred, and from thy father's house, unto a land that I will shew thee: And I will make of thee a great nation, and I will bless thee, and make thy name great; and thou shalt be a blessing: And I will bless them that bless thee, and curse him that curseth thee: and in thee shall all families of the earth be blessed. So Abram departed, as Yahweh had spoken unto him; and Lot went with him: and Abram was seventy and five years old when he departed out of Haran".*

From the narrative, we see that Abraham believed Yahweh and manifested the belief in Yahweh as obedience to His command. Abraham displayed his obedience by embarking on a journey of faith.

Now, we observe that both Paul and James quoted the same scriptures to make different points. However, the position of James is correct and true while that of Paul is wrong and false. This deduction is clear from Yahweh's testimony in Genesis 22:16-18;

*"And said, By myself have I sworn, saith Yahweh, for because thou hast done this thing, and hast not withheld thy son, thine only son: That in blessing I will bless thee, and in multiplying I will multiply thy seed as the stars of the heaven, and as the sand which is upon the sea shore; and thy seed shall possess the gate of his enemies; And in thy seed shall all the nations of the earth be blessed; <u>because thou hast obeyed my voice</u>".*

Yahweh testifies here again that Abraham not only believed Him but Abraham OBEYED His commandment. He did that which he was told to do; therefore, the righteousness of Abraham did not stem from mere belief or just believing Yahweh but also from <u>obeying the voice and doing the will of Yahweh.</u>

Always remember that whatever the case may be, that in every step of the journey, Yahweh is teaching us something. Meanwhile, the Law of Yahweh is a protective barrier to keep the obedient believers from the reaches and realms of the adversary who is Satan and his angels. If we have this understanding as believers, we will know what to do as the psalmist stated in Psalms 119:34; *"Give me understanding, and I shall keep thy law; yea, I shall observe it with my whole heart".*

# MONEY OR THE LOVE OF MONEY IS NOT THE ROOT OF ALL EVIL

Paul wrote to his convert Timothy in his letter 1 Timothy 6:10; *"For the Love of Money is the Root of All Evil: which while some coveted after, they have erred from the faith, and pierced themselves through with many sorrows"*.

However, from the Scriptures, we can deduce that evil began with Satan the angel previously known as Lucifer. Money or the love of money was not the cause of his evil, iniquity and fall; rather, the Scriptures record in the prophecy of Isaiah 14:12-15;

*"How art thou fallen from heaven, O Lucifer, son of the morning! how art thou cut down to the ground, which didst weaken the nations! For thou hast said in thine heart, I will ascend into heaven, I will exalt my throne above the stars of El: I will sit also upon the mount of the congregation, in the sides of the north: I will ascend above the heights of the clouds; I will be like the most High. Yet thou shalt be brought down to hell, to the sides of the pit"*.

Here, we discover that the energy and condition behind **Sin** is **Pride** and **not Money**. This makes pride the root of all evil and renders this popular statement of Paul to Timothy and other believers about the love for money being the root of all evil an obvious error.

Also, we can read and glean from Proverbs 16:18; *"Pride goeth before destruction, and a haughty spirit before a fall."*

And Proverbs 8:13; *"The fear of the LORD is to hate evil: Pride, and arrogancy, and the evil way, and the froward mouth, do I hate."*

Paul also wrote to Timothy later, while designating the attributes of a man who is fit for the office of a Bishop, in 1 Timothy 3:6; ***"Not a novice, lest <u>being lifted up with pride he fall into the condemnation of the devil.</u>"***

Paul ought to understand that money was never involved in the condemnation of the devil and therefore the love of money is not the root of all evils.

Also, from the Scriptures, we read that Cain killed his brother Abel in a fit of rage. The murder of a brother is evil no doubt. However, money was not involved in the thought, predetermination and, execution of the evil deed by Cain. See Genesis 4:8; ***"And Cain talked with Abel his brother: and it came to pass, when they were in the field, that Cain rose up against Abel his brother, and slew him"***.

# A WRONG QUOTATION

In the letter of Paul to the congregation in Ephesus, he wrote in Ephesians 5:14; *"Wherefore he saith, Awake thou that sleepest, and arise from the dead, and the Messiah shall give thee light"*.

This is a misquoting of the Scriptures from the prophecy of Isaiah in Isaiah 60:1-2;

*"Arise, shine; for thy light is come, and the glory of Yahweh is risen upon thee. For, behold, the darkness shall cover the earth, and gross darkness the people: but Yahweh shall arise upon thee, and his glory shall be seen upon thee"*.

When we quote any part of the Holy Scriptures to support a teaching or doctrine, we must quote it verbatim to show ourselves as faithful witnesses of the Spirit of Yahweh and ministers of the Truth. Also, we do so to establish the point we want to make as scripturally correct, Spiritually true and confirmable.

# ALL THE LAW

Another error from Paul is found in his letter to the congregation in Galatia where he wrote in Galatians 5:14; *"For all the law is fulfilled in one word, even in this; Thou shalt love thy neighbor as thyself."*

Note the statement "All the Law is fulfilled in one word". According to Paul, this means the whole Law is fulfilled in one commandment and that commandment is "Thou shalt love thy neighbor as thyself". Paul's position here is, in fact, an error because it is contrary to the position held by the Master. Our Master Yahshua Messiah talked about and confirmed another separate commandment greater than the commandment presented by Paul. Our Master Yahshua Messiah made this clear when a lawyer asked him (Yahshua Messiah) a question about this matter in the Gospel according to Matthew in Matthew 22:36-38;

*"Rabbi, which is the great commandment in the law? Yahshua said unto him, Thou shalt love YAHWEH thy Elohim with all thy heart, and with all thy soul, and with all thy mind. This is the first and great commandment".*

The Master Yahshua Messiah made it clear that the most important commandment is the commandment to love Yahweh Elohim with all of one's heart, soul, mind and strength of a believer. The Master places the commandment to love one's neighbour as one's self in the second place.

See Mark 12:30-31;

*"And thou shalt love Yahweh thy Elohim with all thy heart, and with all thy soul, and with all thy mind, and with all thy strength: this is the first commandment. And the second is like, namely this, Thou shalt love thy neighbour as thyself. There is no other commandment greater than these.*

Obviously, Paul was never present at the Master's teachings and that is why, in his letter, he made this error of taking the second commandment as the embodiment of the whole Law of Yahweh to the Galatian congregation.

# WHERE THERE IS NO LAW

Paul wrote in his letter to the Roman congregation in Romans 4:15; *"Because the law worketh wrath: for where no law is, there is no transgression."*

Prophet Nathan Ben Ragshi modify this statement as a prophet of Yahshua Messiah and I say, "Where there is no Law, there is Lawlessness".

Paul went further to write to the Roman congregation in Romans 5:13; *(For until the law sin was in the world: but sin is not imputed when there is no law.)*

I say this is another error because there was punishment for sinfulness and wickedness before the Law was given through Moses. The flood in Noah's days is a case in point as we read in the Scriptures of Genesis 6:5-7;

*"And Elohim saw that the wickedness of man was great in the earth, and that every imagination of the thoughts of his heart was only evil continually. And it repented Yahweh that he had made man on the earth, and it grieved him at his heart. And Yahweh said, I will destroy man whom I have created from the face of the earth; both man, and beast, and the creeping thing, and the fowls of the air; for it repenteth me that I have made them".*

Also, we see the consequence of sin in the overthrowing of Sodom, Gomorrah and the neighbouring cities as we read in Genesis 18:20-21;

*"And Yahweh said, Because the cry of Sodom and Gomorrah is great, and because their sin is very grievous; I will go down now, and see whether they have done altogether according to the cry of it, which is come unto me; and if not, I will know".*

Genesis 19:24-25;

*"Then Yahweh rained upon Sodom and upon Gomorrah brimstone and*

**_fire from Yahweh out of heaven; and He overthrew those cities, and all the plain, and all the inhabitants of the cities, and that which grew upon the ground"._**

We see that there was punishment for sin and wickedness before the Law was given. Hence, to say that Sin was not charged or imputed before the Law is erroneous.

# THE LAW, THE ENMITY;

Paul wrote again to the congregation in Ephesus in Ephesians 2:15;

*"Having abolished in his flesh the enmity, even the law of commandments contained in ordinances; for to make in himself of twain one new man, so making peace;"*

I took time to meditate on this statement made by Paul and I asked: "When did the Law become the enmity between the Jews and the Gentiles? Was the law the cause of the enslavement of Israel in Egypt? Was the Law the cause of the contention between Israel and the Canaanite nations occupying the land of Canaan?"

Interestingly, the Master Yahshua Messiah declared unequivocally in the Gospel according to Matthew in Matthew 5:17-18;

*"Think not that I am come to destroy the law, or the prophets: I am not come to destroy, but to fulfill. For verily I say unto you, till heaven and earth pass, one jot or one tittle shall in no wise pass from the law, till all be fulfilled."*

So, the Law was never abolished; hence, Paul's statement is a dangerous error. He was bound to make the error as he did not receive any teaching from the Master Yahshua Messiah physically like the twelve Apostles and other disciples of Yahshua Messiah.

Some false believers and false teachers, who are inclined towards rebellion and disobedience, will say that the Master has fulfilled the Law. However, in reality, no law anywhere is made to be fulfilled at any time. Rather, laws are meant to be continually and continuously obeyed until they are abolished.

Observe Matthew 5:17-18 closely:

*"Think not that I am come to destroy the law, or the prophets: I am not come to destroy, but to fulfill. For verily I say unto you, till heaven and*

***earth pass, one jot or one tittle shall in no wise pass from the law, till all be fulfilled".***

In the passage, the Master talked about two aspects of the Scriptures which are the Law and the Prophets. Then, He uses two verb words which are: 'fulfil' and 'establish'. A sincere mind will understand that prophecies are meant to be fulfilled whereas laws are either established or abolished. Therefore, the Master is saying that He came to <u>fulfil the prophecies</u> while <u>establishing the Laws</u> of His Father is also part of the assignment. So, Paul was in error once again in this part of his teachings and doctrine.

Moreover, every Gentile convert and believer in Yahshua Messiah has technically been grafted into the nation or commonwealth of Israel, because Yahshua Messiah is the King of Israel sitting on the throne of David, which throne we know has become heavenly. Also, the Scriptures clarify that there was to be always one law for the home-born Israelites and strangers or foreigners — see Exodus 12:49; ***"One law shall be to him that is homeborn, and unto the stranger that sojourneth among you."***

## GIFTS OF GOD WITHOUT REPENTANCE;

Paul wrote again to the Roman congregation in Romans 11:29; ***"For the gifts and calling of God are without repentance".*** (KJV)

***"For the gifts and calling of Yahweh are without repentance".*** (HNB)

This is a false and erroneous statement, because the Scriptures tell us that Adam lost the Garden of Eden, Eli lost the priesthood, Samson lost his strength, Saul lost the kingdom, Israel lost the Promised Land, and we can go on and on. The Psalmist prayed Psalm 51:11; ***"Cast me not away from thy presence; and take not thy holy spirit from me."***

If the gift of the Holy Spirit cannot be retrieved, why would the psalmist pray such a prayer by the Spirit? It is impossible for the gifts and calling of Yahweh to remain with a backslider who has returned to being a sinner. We may consider the Scriptures of 1 Samuel 16:14 "Now the Spirit of Yahweh departed from Saul, and an evil spirit from Yahweh troubled him".

# WHO TO FOLLOW;

Paul wrote to the congregation in Thessalonians in 2 Thessalonians 3:6;

*"Now we command you, brethren, in the name of our Master Yahshua the Messiah, that ye withdraw yourselves from every brother that walketh disorderly, and not after the tradition which he received of us".*

However, as believers, we ought to follow the commandments of Yahweh Elohim and of our Saviour Yahshua Messiah, not after the tradition of men be it Paul or Apollos or any other self-acclaimed apostle, prophet, evangelist or teacher.

Yahshua Messiah questioned the Pharisees in the Gospel according to Matthew in Matthew 15:3 thus: *"But he answered and said unto them, Why do ye also transgress the commandment of Yahweh by your tradition"?*

## FAITH AND THE LAW;

Paul wrote in his letter to the congregation in Galatia in Galatians 3:2; *"This only would I learn of you, Received ye the Spirit by the works of the law, or by the hearing of faith?"*

In this statement, the hearing of faith is a complex statement. See what Paul wrote to the Roman congregation in Romans 10:17; *"So then faith cometh by hearing, and hearing by the word of Yahweh."*

Now, the Word of Yahweh consists of the Law, the Prophets and the Gospels. Regarding the Law, Paul says in Romans 2:13; (For not the hearers of the law are just before Yahweh, but the doers of the law shall be justified.).

James the brother of our Messiah also states in his letter James 1:22; *"But be ye doers of the word, and not hearers only, deceiving your own selves."*

The Law is part of the Word of Yahweh. Hence, to be effective as a believer and part of the Kingdom, you must be a doer of the commandments. The Spirit enables the believer to do the Law. This position is confirmed by the Master in the Gospel of Matthew in Matthew 7:21; *"Not every one that saith unto me, Lord, Lord, shall enter into the kingdom of heaven; but he that doeth the will of my Father which is in heaven."*

The will of the Father is outlined in the Law, the Prophets and the Gospels.


## NOW, WHAT IS FAITH?

The English dictionary defines faith as a firm belief in God, doctrines or something of which there is no proof.

However, in the letter to the Hebrews, the writer defines faith in Hebrews 11:1; *"Now faith is the substance of things hoped for, the evidence of things not seen".*

These definitions are not perfect concerning the Scriptures. Therefore, by the Word of Yahweh, I Nathan Ben Ragshi a prophet of Yahshua Messiah define Faith thus; **Faith is the correct and proper understanding of what is believed".** From this definition, we see that there is a difference between Belief and Faith and the difference is that most valuable ability or power called '**understanding**'. Once again, remember the words of the wise king Solomon in Proverbs 4:7; *"Wisdom is the principal thing; therefore get wisdom: and with all thy getting get understanding."*

Another version says: *"The beginning of wisdom is this: Get wisdom. Though it cost all you have, get understanding."*

Therefore, faith is a matter of understanding. The beloved Apostle John wrote in his Epistle to the believers in 1 John 5:20;

*"And we know that the Son of Yahweh is come, and hath given us an UNDERSTANDING, that we may know him that is true, and we are in him that is true, even in his Son Yahshua the Messiah. This is the true Elohim, and eternal life."*

## RIGHTEOUSNESS, SIN AND GRACE;

Master Yahshua Messiah spoke profoundly in the Gospel according to Apostle John in John 16:7-8;

*"But very truly I tell you, it is for your good that I am going away. Unless I go away, the Advocate will not come to you; but if I go, I will send him to you. When he comes, he will prove the world to be in the wrong about sin and righteousness and judgment":*

## NOW WHAT IS SIN?

Sin is clearly defined by Apostle John in his first Epistle — 1 John.3:4; *"__Whosoever committeth Sin Transgresseth also the Law: <u>for Sin is the Transgression of the Law</u>__".*

Therefore, Sin is not about what we perceive to be evil or wrong but a transgression of the Law of Yahweh. In human nature, there is the tendency to use the Law wrongfully; that also is SIN.

Righteousness, on the other hand, is doing what is right in the sight of Yahweh and that is according to His laws, commandments, statutes, precepts and judgments. Hence, <u>Righteousness is Obedience without Sin.</u>

## GRACE

Grace is divine favour from Yahweh. As humans already fallen in nature, we do not merit it, yet Yahweh gives it to us freely. However, since the Master Yahshua Messiah talked about Judgment, the related word should be Mercy since Mercy is compassion or forbearance shown especially to an offender or a sinner by an authority.

Yahweh introduced himself officially to Moses in Exodus 34:6-7;

*"And Yahweh passed by before him, and proclaimed, Yahweh, Yahweh-El, merciful and gracious, long-suffering, and abundant in goodness and truth, Keeping mercy for thousands, forgiving iniquity and transgression*

*and sin, and that will by no means clear the guilty; visiting the iniquity of the fathers upon the children, and upon the children's children, unto the third and to the fourth generation".*

We see that Yahweh is merciful and gracious. Meanwhile, mercy is for forgiving iniquity, transgression and sin.

## THE LAW OF SIN AND DEATH

Paul wrote to the Roman congregation in Romans 8:2; *"For the law of the Spirit of life in Messiah Yahshua hath made me free from the law of sin and death."*

Now, there is only one law and it is the Law of Yahweh. Since Yahweh is a Life-giving Spirit, the Law of Yahweh is <u>the Law of the Spirit of Life.</u> As stated in Leviticus 18:5; *"You shall therefore <u>keep my statutes and my ordinances;</u> which if a man does, he <u>shall live</u> in them. I am Yahweh."*

There is no other Law of Sin and Death, because sin is the transgression of the Law of Yahweh, and the consequences and wages of sin is death.

## ONLY ONE SIN AGAINST THE BODY

Paul wrote to the congregation in Corinth in 1 Corinthians 6:18 saying: *"Flee fornication. Every sin that a man doeth is without the body; but he that committeth fornication sinneth against his own body"*

This also is an error because we may ask; "What sins are outside the body?" Adultery, idolatry, stealing, murders, covetousness, greed, gluttony...? The reality is that No sin is without the body. The Master Yahshua Messiah explains this in the Gospel according to Matthew in Matthew 15:19; *"For out of the heart proceed evil thoughts, murders, adulteries, fornications, thefts, false witness, blasphemies: These are the things which defile a man:"*

All sins committed with the body and are against the body, for the soul that sinneth shall die.

## NO DISTINCTION IN THE KINGDOM

The idea that, once you are a believer, there is no distinguishing or distinction in the Kingdom is another dangerous error from Paul. Paul wrote to the congregation in Galatia; Galatians 3:27-28;

*"For as many of you as have been baptized into the Messiah have put on the Messiah. There is neither Jew nor Greek, there is neither bond nor free, there is neither male nor female: for ye are all one in the Messiah Yahshua."*

As a convert, there is one Messiah just as there is one Law, but there are specific instructions for a man, a woman, a home-born Jew, a Gentile convert, a husband, a wife, a virgin, a parent, a child, etc, otherwise believers become stateless, androgynous, cryptogenic and transgender beings and this cannot be the case presently until after the resurrection.

Perhaps Paul was trying to say there is no distinction in the invitation to the Kingdom as all are invited, Jews, and Greeks, men, and women, old and young. However, once you come into the Kingdom, you must find your position and act accordingly depending on who you are and your position as designated in the Kingdom.

Again, Paul wrote to the Roman congregation in Romans 14:1-4;

*"Him that is weak in the faith receive ye, but not to doubtful disputations. For one believeth that he may eat all things: another, who is weak, eateth herbs. Let not him that eateth despise him that eateth not; and let not him which eateth not judge him that eateth: for Yahweh hath received him. Who art thou that judgest another man?s servant? to his own master he standeth or falleth. Yea, he shall be holden up: for Yahweh is able to make him stand".*

We cannot live as believers based on our personal beliefs and opinions. This is the origin of false believers, false prophets, false apostles, false teachers and all manner of falsehood. An aspect of the Law of Yahweh concerns nutrition and clean and unclean foods. Meanwhile, Yahweh concludes in Leviticus 11:44;

*"For I am Yahweh your Elohim: ye shall therefore sanctify yourselves, and ye shall be holy; for I am holy: neither shall ye defile yourselves with any manner of creeping thing that creepeth upon the earth."*

Yahweh is the same as when he gave the Law, even today and forever. In Matthew 5:18, Yahshua Messiah stated: *"For verily I say unto you, Till heaven and earth pass, one jot or one tittle shall in no wise pass from the law, till all be fulfilled."*

This means nothing changes from the Law until all the prophecies are fulfilled. Part of the prophecies to the fulfilled is "A new heaven and a new earth" as in Isaiah 65:17; *"For, behold, I create new heavens and a new earth: and the former shall not be remembered, nor come into mind".*

That is why the Master stated that until this present heaven and earth pass away according to prophets, the Law of Yahweh remains unchanged.


## THE SABBATH DAY

Paul wrote another error in his letter to the congregation in Rome in Romans14:5-6;

*"One man esteemeth one day above another: another esteemeth every day alike. Let every man be fully persuaded in his own mind. He that regardeth the day, regardeth it unto Yahweh; and he that regardeth not the day, to Yahweh he doth not regard it. He that eateth, eateth to Yahweh, for he giveth Yahweh thanks; and he that eateth not, to Yahweh he eateth not, and giveth Yahweh thanks."*

Here, Paul undermines the Law of Yahweh concerning certain days as well as certain diets. He seems to conclude that they are acceptable to Yahweh as long as one gives thanks to Him. Now, let it be understood that, giving thanks to Yahweh is a form of sacrifice or offering. Let's consider once again what the Word of Yahweh says concerning sacrifices and offerings — 1Samuel 15:22-23;

*"And Samuel said, <u>Hath Yahweh as great delight in burnt offerings and sacrifices, as in obeying the voice of Yahweh? Behold, to obey is better</u>*

*than sacrifice, and to <u>hearken than the fat of rams</u>. For rebellion is as the sin of witchcraft, and stubbornness is as iniquity and idolatry. Because thou hast rejected the word of Yahweh, he hath also rejected thee from being king".*

From this scripture, we see that it is more acceptable to Yahweh that we obey His commandments than to give thanks and praises to Him, because thanks, praises and other forms of sacrifices become acceptable to Yahweh only when they are based on obedience to His commandments.

Let's examine the commandment concerning the Sabbath days. There are certain days that Yahweh commanded His subjects in His Law to keep as holy to Him; the first of such Sabbaths is the seventh and last day of the week. All over the world, Sunday is accepted as the first day of the week; therefore, the last day will be Saturday. That makes Saturday the seventh and last day of the week, making it the Sabbath day.

Concerning this seventh day, the Scriptures record in Genesis 2:2-3;

*"And on the seventh day Elohim ended his work which he had made; and he rested on the seventh day from all his work which he had made. And Elohim blessed the seventh day, and sanctified it: because that in it he had rested from all his work which Elohim created and made."*

This historical fact is impossible to change. Even if there is permission to edit and modify the Law, the facts of truth and history cannot be changed or modified. Also, we have established, from the Words of Yahshua Messiah our Master, that there will be no changes to the Law until the end of times.

In the Law of Yahweh, Yahweh commanded Exodus 20:8-11;

*"Remember the sabbath day, to keep it holy. Six days shalt thou labour, and do all thy work: But the seventh day is the sabbath of Yahweh thy Elohim: in it thou shalt not do any work, thou, nor thy son, nor thy daughter, thy manservant, nor thy maidservant, nor thy cattle, nor thy stranger that is within thy gates: For in six days Yahweh made heaven and earth, the sea, and all that in them is, and rested the seventh day: wherefore Yahweh blessed the sabbath day, and hallowed it."*

Yahweh commands again in Exodus 31:13;

*"Speak thou also unto the children of Israel, saying, Verily my sabbaths ye shall keep: for it is a sign between me and you throughout your generations; that ye may know that I am Yahweh that doth sanctify you."*

Hence, we see that Yahweh gave the Sabbath to be kept as a sign to represent the complex notion of a covenant between Yahweh Elohim and his subjects. Yahweh gave the Sabbath to man to keep. Note that Yahweh did not give man to the Sabbath; rather, He gave the Sabbath to man. That is the reason for the Master Yahshua Messiah's statement in Mark 2:27; *"And he said unto them, The sabbath was made for man, and not man for the sabbath:"*

The Sabbath was made for man means the Sabbath was given to man and if the Sabbath was given to man to keep, it becomes a sin if the man doesn't keep it accordingly. See Exodus 31:14;

*"Ye shall keep the sabbath therefore; for it is holy unto you: every one that defileth it shall surely be put to death: for whosoever doeth any work therein, that soul shall be cut off from among his people."*

In the Prophets, the Scriptures record concerning the Sabbath days as in Isaiah 56:2;

*"Blessed is the man that doeth this, and the son of man that layeth hold on it; that keepeth the sabbath from polluting it, and keepeth his hand from doing any evil."*

It becomes irrefutable that, without the Law, we cannot know the Sabbath days and be a partaker of Yahweh's blessing for keeping them. Again, we see the more blessings of Yahweh in the prophecy of Isaiah in Isaiah 56:4-5;

*"For thus saith the LORD unto the eunuchs that keep my sabbaths, and choose the things that please me, and take hold of my covenant; Even unto them will I give in mine house and within my walls a place and a name better than of sons and of daughters: I will give them an everlasting name, that shall not be cut off".*

Yahweh in the scripture blesses the Eunuch who keeps his Sabbaths. Of course, not all of us can be eunuchs even as the Master Yahshua Messiah stated in the Gospel of Matthew in Matthew 19:11-12;

*"But he said unto them, All men cannot receive this saying, save they to whom it is given. For there are some eunuchs, which were so born from their mother's womb: and there are some eunuchs, which were made eunuchs of men: and there be eunuchs, which have made themselves eunuchs for the kingdom of heaven's sake. He that is able to receive it, let him receive it".*

There are still more blessings indicated by Yahweh to be bestowed on His faithfuls as stated in the Scriptures of the Prophets in Isaiah 56:6-7;

*"Also the foreigners who join themselves to Yahweh, to minister to him, and to love Yahweh's name, to be his servants, everyone who keeps the Sabbath from profaning it, and holds fast my covenant; even them will I bring to my holy mountain, and make them joyful in my house of prayer: their burnt offerings and their sacrifices shall be accepted on my altar; for my house shall be called a house of prayer for all peoples."*

So, Yahweh, in this prophecy delivered through Prophet Isaiah, recognized the fact that foreigners who are non-Jews and non-Israelites will come into the Faith, making another distinction in the body of Messiah. Yahweh blessed such initiated foreigners for loving and hallowing His name, for their service in keeping His Sabbaths and holding the New Covenant as mediated by Yahshua Messiah our Master.

Observe that though there was a New Covenant established by the perfect sacrifice offered by Yahshua our Messiah, there was NO abolishment of the Law that was given through Moses neither was any new law written. Rather, there were modifications and additions made to the Law of Yahweh that was given through Moses, which is now sealed by the blood and earthly life of Yahshua Messiah. The modifications to the Law of Yahweh are all extractible from the Scriptures of the Law and the Prophets, many of which functions of prophecy have already been fulfilled by Yahshua Messiah.

The blood of Yahshua was shed for the remission of sins in the New Covenant, and sin remains the transgression of Yahweh's Law. Yahshua Messiah spoke of this while he kept the last Sabbath day of His earthly Life and ministry as seen in the Gospel of Matthew in Matthew 26:27-28;

**"And he took the cup, and gave thanks, and gave it to them, saying, Drink ye all of it; For this is my blood of the New Covenant, which is shed for many for the remission of sins."**

One of the purposes of forgiveness is to enable the forgiven sinner to have another chance to live righteously by doing what is right in the sight of Yahweh as written in the Word of Yahweh, which consists of the Law, the Prophets and the Gospel of Yahshua Messiah. The letters of Paul, although a part of the Bible today, are not a part of the Gospel of Yahshua Messiah since Paul did not know Yahshua Messiah physically in His earthly life. Paul did not know of or witness His teachings, miracles, suffering, death and resurrection first-hand.

Therefore, Paul's letters are expressions of Paul's own understanding and revelation which can be tested just as a believer should test every spirit and also test the Spirit speaking presently through the writer of this publication the Prophet Nathan Ben Ragshi. When the spirit behind doctrines and teachings are tested with Yahweh's Word, they may be found correct or erroneous according to the Word of Yahweh. Paul did not write from the memory of a physical experience of the fact of the earthly life of the Master Yahshua Messiah as witnessed by the original twelve Apostles and other disciples and also as contained in the available Gospels and epistles of the actual Apostles of Yahshua Messiah.

The letters of Paul are not a part of the Law, which was already given by Moses. Also, Paul's letters are not a part of the Prophets as Yahshua Messiah confirmed in the Gospel according to Luke in Luke16:16; **"The law and the prophets were until John: since that time the kingdom of Yahweh, is preached, and every man treats it with contempt".**

This means that the work of the prophets of Yahweh ended with John the 'Immerser' or Baptist. To claim to be a prophet of Yahweh (Man of God) after John the 'Immerser' is questionable unless you are a prophet of Yahshua Messiah. See what Yahshua said in the Gospel according to Matthew in Matthew 11:27;

*"All things are delivered unto me of my Father: and no man knoweth the Son, but the Father; neither knoweth any man the Father, save the Son, and he to whomsoever the Son will reveal him".*

The whole administration and operation of the cosmic system is handed over to the Master Yahshua Messiah as stated in Matthew 28:18; *"And Yahshua came and spake unto them, saying, All power is given unto me in heaven and in earth."*

## NOT WITNESSED BY THE LAW.

Paul wrote to the congregation in Rome in Romans.3:21; *"But now the righteousness of Yahweh without the law is manifested, being witnessed by the law and the prophets";*

However, this is another grievous error as there is no suggestion of this lawless righteousness in the Law or the writings of the Prophets. Rather, we have a clear confirmation that the righteousness of Yahweh Elohim is according to His Law as witnessed in Psalms 119:142; *"Thy righteousness is an everlasting righteousness, and thy law is the truth.*

Also, the Prophet Isaiah records in Isaiah 42:21; *"It pleased Yahweh, for his righteousness' sake, to magnify the law, and make it honorable."*

This means that Yahweh intends to glorify and increase the respect and significance of His Law. Prophet Isaiah goes on, in his prophecy of the word of Yahweh, to record in Isaiah 51:7; *"Hearken unto me, ye that know righteousness, the people in whose heart is my law; fear ye not the reproach of men, neither be ye afraid of their revilings".*

Hence, Paul's idea that a lawless righteousness is witnessed by the Law and the Prophets is a lie and an error.

Also, there is a fault in Paul's suggestion in his letter to the Roman congregation in Romans 2:26; *"Therefore if the uncircumcision keep the righteousness of the law, shall not his uncircumcision be counted for circumcision?*

This is another erroneous utterance because the covenant with Yahweh begins with the circumcision. Hence, any uncircumcised cannot begin to express the righteousness of the Law. This is obvious from Exodus 12:48;

*"And when a stranger shall sojourn with thee, and will keep the Passover to Yahweh, let all his males be circumcised, and then let him come near and keep it; and he shall be as one that is born in the land: for no uncircumcised person shall eat thereof."*

Yahshua Messiah is the Lamb of Yahweh our Passover as recorded in the Gospel of John 1:29; *"The next day John seeth Yeshua coming unto him, and saith, Behold the Lamb of Yahweh, which taketh away the sin of the world"*.

The forgiveness of sins is not the same as the abolishment of the Law. Sin is forgiven so that the sinner can go and sin no more, not for the forgiven sinner to become lawless.

# THE LETTER AND THE SPIRIT

Paul wrote again in his letter to the congregation in Rome in Romans 7:6; *"But now we are delivered from the law, that being dead wherein we were held; that we should serve in newness of spirit, and not in the oldness of the letter"*.

In the forgiveness of Yahshua Messiah, we are delivered from the due punishment of our sins, not from the Law but from the judgment. Paul gave an example of a woman who becomes loosed from marriage to her husband once the husband is late. Clearly, the woman is loosed from her dead husband, not from the Law that bound them, or can their children become illegitimate because one of the spouses died? Of course not. The Law is not dead until it is abolished by the giver of the Law. In Matthew 5:18, the Master says: *"For verily I say unto you, Till heaven and earth pass, one jot or one tittle shall in no wise pass from the law, till all be fulfilled."*

Now, this is the relationship between the Spirit and the written Law: Yahweh is a Spirit and a Spirit is fundamentally a principle or set of principles. The principles of Yahweh's Spirit are expressed in the Laws of Yahweh, and Yahweh is the same ages ago, yesterday, today and forever. Hence, the newness of the Spirit is not the discarding of the Law of Yahweh. Rather, it is the understanding of the Law through our Master Yahshua Messiah who gave us the understanding. See 1John 5:20;

*"And we know that the Son of Yahweh is come, and hath given us an understanding, that we may know him that is true, and we are in him that is true, even in his Son Yahshua the Messiah. This is the true Elohim, and eternal life.* Psalms.119:142 *Thy righteousness is an everlasting righteousness and <u>thy law is the truth</u>.*

Yahshua Messiah is the Truth and, therefore, the <u>Law of Yahweh</u> which is contained in the <u>Word of Yahweh</u>. The Word of Yahweh became flesh and dwelt among men in the person of Yahshua Messiah — John.1:14; *"And the*

*Word was made flesh, and dwelt among us, (and we beheld his glory, the glory as of the only begotten of the Father,) full of grace and truth."*

In John 6:63, Yahshua Messiah says: *"It is the Spirit that quickeneth the flesh; but ye say the flesh profiteth nothing: the words that I speak unto you, they are Spirit, and they are life."*

Paul, approbating and reprobating, stated in Romans 7:12; *"Wherefore the law is holy and the commandment holy, and just, and good".*

Also, in Romans 7:14, Paul said: *"For we know that the law is spiritual: but I am carnal, sold under sin."*

People talk about Logos and Rhema, these are terms that represent the written Law and the spiritual revelation respectively, but they forget the Son of Man who is the Word in the flesh. Here are <u>the three essential parts of the Word of Yahweh</u>:

1. <u>The Letter</u> made of <u>the Law and the Prophets</u>

2. The Son of Man being the Word in the Flesh that is the person of Yahshua the Messiah

3. The Spirit of Truth which is the Holy Spirit

These three bear witness of the Truth and agree in one.

Paul wrote in Romans 7:8; *"But sin, taking occasion by the commandment, wrought in me all manner of concupiscence. For without the law sin was dead".*

That Sin is dead without the Law is an error. Rather, sin is unknown, so where there is no Law, the sinner is not aware of the sinful nature of his/her action.

Consider Romans 7:9; *"For I was alive without the law once: but when the commandment came, sin revived, and I died".*

This again is an error because Adam was alive with the commandment but committed sin by disobedience and died according to the Word of Yahweh. Now, man was spiritually dead (as inherited from Adam) until the Law was given. According to Yahweh, the Law can give life — Leviticus 18:5; *"You shall therefore keep my statutes and my ordinances; which if a man does, he shall live in them. I am Yahweh."*

See also Proverbs 6:23; *"For the commandment is a lamp; and the law is light; and reproofs of instruction are the way of life":*

Paul, in his letter to the congregation in Rome, said this in Romans.7:25; *"Thanks be to Yahweh through Yahshua the Messiah our Saviour. So then with the mind I myself serve the law of Yahweh; but with the flesh the law of sin".*

The question here is what is the Law of Sin and how is it different from the Law of Yahweh? This statement is questionable.


## ALL THINGS LAWFUL

Paul wrote this to the congregation in Corinth in 1 Corinthians 6:12; *"All things are lawful unto me, but all things are not expedient: all things are lawful for me, but I will not be brought under the power of any".*

This is an erroneous statement in comparison with the Words of Yahweh in the Old Covenant Scriptures and also with the Words of the Master Yahshua Messiah in the Gospels of the New Covenant. Also, it is erroneous because all things cannot be lawful even in a lawless state.

Also, in Paul's writing in 1 Corinthians 5:5, he said: *"To deliver such an one unto Satan for the destruction of the flesh, that the spirit may be saved in the day of the Master Yahshua".*

How do you deliver a person to Satan? The Kingdom of Yahweh and Yahshua Messiah has no business of delivering and exchanging people with the Kingdom of Satan. Paul could have said to expel the sinner from the congregation, which Yahweh, in His Law, refers to as being "cut off" from the congregation of His people.

Paul writes this to the congregation in Corinth in 1 Corinthians 7:19; *"Circumcision is nothing, and uncircumcision is nothing, but the keeping of the commandments of Yahweh"*.

This is an error because, once again, every command of Yahweh means a lot and keeping the Commandments and obeying the Laws of Yahweh is everything. Meanwhile, the circumcision of every male is the beginning of the Covenant with Yahweh.

Another error is contained in Paul's letter to the congregation in Corinth in 1 Corinthians 8:1; *"Now as touching things offered unto idols, we know that we all have knowledge. Knowledge puffeth up, but love edifieth"*.

The Truth is that <u>knowledge does not puff up</u>; knowledge disciplines the mind. However, <u>pride, when mixed with ignorance, puffs up</u> the mind of the ignorant.

Also, in the letter of Paul to the congregation in Corinth, Paul asked in 1Corinthians 9:1-2;

*"Am I not an apostle? am I not free? have I not seen Yahshua the Messiah our Master? are not ye my work in Yahweh? If I be not an apostle unto others, yet doubtless I am to you: for the seal of mine apostleship are ye in Yahweh"*.

The right answers to Paul's questions are: "No, Mr. Paul, you are not an Apostle but an Evangelist. You did not see, meet or hear the Master Yahshua Messiah physically during His earthly ministry. Your work and seal is that of evangelism. You cannot make yourself an Apostle of Yahshua Messiah to some and at the same time not be an apostle to others, because an Apostle is an apostle not to any set of people but of the one and only Master Yahshua Messiah. Also, an Apostle is appointed by the Master Yahshua Messiah in the presence of witnesses consisting of other Apostles and disciples."

Therefore, I Prophet Nathan Ben Ragshi a prophet of Yahshua Messiah say unequivocally that Paul is an Evangelist and not an Apostle of Yahshua Messiah!

## BEING A PROPHET

Paul had this to say to the congregation in Corinth in 1 Corinthians 14:37; *"If any man think himself to be a prophet, or spiritual, let him acknowledge that the things that I write unto you are the commandments of the Lord"*.

If a man is a prophet by the Master's calling, then he is a Prophet indeed. However, if a man just assumes or thinks that he is a prophet, then he is most likely a false prophet. If there were commandments given, they must be from the Scriptures, either from the Law, the Prophets or the Gospels.

Paul is not a Lawgiver; therefore, any commandments from Paul or any other person that don't originate from the Scriptures cannot be accepted as a commandment from Yahweh or from Yahshua Messiah to the Church.

Of course, women are meant to remain silent in the administration of the Kingdom and mysteries of Yahweh. This is so because, first, the woman was first to be deceived by the devil. She was used by the devil to achieve his aim of killing the man by getting him to disobey the commandment of Yahweh.

Yahweh Elohim the Creator commanded Adam not to eat the fruit of the tree of the knowledge of good and evil before the woman was created. Technically the man therefore is the actual victim of the sin. Therefore, the redemption plan and arrangement are for and about the man. This is evident from the command of circumcision where we see that only the males were to be circumcised in Genesis 17:10; *"This is my covenant, which ye shall keep, between me and you and thy seed after thee; Every man child among you shall be circumcised."*

The covenant, therefore, does not involve women. It is a blood covenant between Yahweh and Abraham involving the only Begotten Son of Yahweh and the Sons of Abraham. The whole operation is a blood covenant confraternity between the only Begotten Son of Yahweh and the sons of Abraham established by the circumcision and sealed by the crucifixion of the Master Yahshua Messiah. That is why in the Priesthood of Aaron, there were no Priestesses and in the Kingship of David or Israel, there were no ruling queens except Jezebel and her daughter Athalia. In the Scriptures, we have no books written by women or by a Prophetess. Finally, the Master Yahshua Messiah did not elect any female Apostle, disciples or Prophetesses despite the evidence that there were many women who followed Him and ministered to Him of their substance.

Women are not meant to preach or teach the mysteries of a Covenant that they are not directly involved in. Any woman insisting on preaching or teaching the mysteries of the Kingdom of Yahweh Elohim and of His Only Begotten Son Yahshua Messiah of Nazareth is rebellious and Jezebelian in her spirit. This position is affirmed by the Master's revelation to John in Revelation 2:20;

***"Notwithstanding I have a few things against thee, because thou sufferest that woman Jezebel, which calleth herself a prophetess, to teach and to seduce my servants to commit fornication, and to eat things sacrificed unto idols."***

In this verse, fornication is of a spiritual nature and dimension and not just engaging in immoral sexual activities. Paul wrote again in 2 Corinthians 3:6; ***"Who also hath made us able ministers of the new testament; not of the letter, but of the spirit: for the letter killeth, but the spirit giveth life".***

This is another error. The letter, which means the written Law, doesn't kill; It is disobedience to the Law which is Sin that kills. Paul wrote in addition in Romans 2:8-9;

***"But unto them that are contentious, and do not obey the truth, but obey unrighteousness, indignation and wrath, Tribulation and anguish, upon every soul of man that doeth evil, of the Jew first, and also of the Gentile;.***

## WE KNOW HIM ACCORDING TO THE SCRIPTURES

In his letter to the church at Corinth, Paul, in 2Corinthians.5:16 said: ***"Wherefore henceforth know we no man after the flesh: yea, though we have known the Messiah after the flesh, yet now henceforth know we him no more".***

How can anyone say we know the Messiah no more? Did we lose our memories? Rather I say authoritatively that we know Him and we continue to know Him much better every day by reading the scriptures and meditating on it with the help of the Holy Spirit. See Psalms 1:1-2;

*"Blessed is the man that walketh not in the counsel of the ungodly, nor standeth in the way of sinners, nor sitteth in the seat of the scornful. But his delight is in the law of the Lord; and in his law doth he meditate day and night".*

## FOOLISH SPEAKING

Writing to the church in Corinth, Paul, in 2 Corinthians 11:17 said: *"That which I speak, I speak it not according to Yahweh, but as it were foolishly, in this confidence of boasting".*

Here, Paul is boasting in an unscriptural way, and this is caused by pride. I say this because, indeed, Paul received a vision of Yahshua Messiah but he didn't go to humble himself before the appointed Apostles so that they might teach him what they learned first-hand from the Master. Instead, Paul relied on his revelations as we may revisit again in Galatians 1:11-13;

*"But I certify you, brethren, that the glad tidings which was preached of me is not after man. For I neither received it of man, neither was I taught it, but by the revelation of Yahshua the Messiah. For ye have heard of my conversation in time past in the Jew's religion, how that beyond measure I persecuted the assembly of Yahweh, and wasted it:* Also Galatians.1:15-17 *"But when it pleased Yahweh, who separated me from my mother's womb, and called me by his grace, To reveal his Son in me, that I might preach him among the heathen; immediately I conferred not with flesh and blood: Neither went I up to Jerusalem to them which were apostles before me; but I went into Arabia, and returned again unto Damascus".*

You cannot know the Messiah fully and wholly just by a spiritual vision and revelation only; you must hear and learn the teachings the Master committed to His appointed and chosen Apostles.

## WITHSTANDING THE APOSTLE PETER

Paul wrote to the congregation in Galatia in Galatians 2:9;

*"And when James, Cephas, and John, <u>who seemed to be pillars</u>, perceived the grace that was given unto me, they gave to me and Barnabas the right hands of fellowship; that we should go unto the heathen, and they unto the circumcision".*

Apostles Peter, being the foremost among the Apostles, is not seemingly one of the pillars. Peter (Cephas, in the above quote), John and James are the Apostles before whom Yahshua Messiah was transfigured on the mountain. The twelve Apostles are the very foundation upon which the Faith is built with Yahshua Messiah being the Chief Corner Stone.

Let's read what Paul wrote in Galatians 2:11; *"But when Peter was come to Antioch, I withstood him to the face, because he was to be blamed".*

Paul wrote this about Apostle Peter but Apostle Peter did not confirm this incident; rather, in his epistle, Apostle Peter wrote this about Paul in 2 Peter 3:15-17;

*"And account that the longsuffering of our Master is salvation; even as our beloved brother Paul also according to the wisdom given unto him hath written unto you; As also in all his epistles, speaking in them of these things; in which are some things hard to be understood, which they that are unlearned and unstable wrest, as they do also the other scriptures, unto their own destruction. Ye therefore, beloved, seeing ye know these things before, beware lest ye also, being led away with the error of the wicked, fall from your own steadfastness".*

Apostle Peter confirms that Paul is a brother. This is evidence of the Master's longsuffering because Paul persecuted the believers previously. Apostle Peter also states that many of the things that Paul wrote are <u>incomprehensible, confusing and unfathomable,</u> and Apostle Peter wisely refers to these contradictions in the writings of Paul as the <u>"error of the wicked"</u>.

# Chapter 4
# THE CLOSURE

# THE INALIENABILITY OF THE LAW

Pinpointing the errors of Paul in this writing is a crucial work of ministry, especially as it affects the Christian church in general. It is clear that Christianity is not a system, religion or Faith that originated just on its own; rather, it is a product of the Jewish faith known as Judaism. Whether or not it is an offspring delivered with congenital anomalies remains to be substantiated using the very text it purports to represent.

It is also important to note that Judaism as the genitor of Christianity did not cease to bear fruits despite the tremendous challenges that Christianity has posed to Judaism due to Christianity's disabilities cerebrally, corporeally and spiritually.

The writer of this book, Nathan Ben Ragshi, being a prophet of the Master Yahshua Messiah of Nazareth serves as a guide to Christians and Christianity, especially those who still have any little desire for what the truth is in every aspect of the Christian Faith and to the other bud of Judaism now called Messianism and Messianics but in times past were called Judaizers (a capital offense) by Christianity, irrespective of the fact that they are of the same parent.

Paul puts himself in the position of a lawgiver but such a role is not needed since Yahshua Messiah the King has already been revealed. The role of giving commands and setting rules for the church or ecclesia that Paul assumed was never prophesied in the Law, the Prophets or in the Gospels.

It is unimaginable that despite the Commandments and Law of Yahweh, Paul still went ahead to write this to the Galatian congregation in Galatians 5:2-6;

*"Behold, I Paul say unto you, that if ye be circumcised, the Messiah shall profit you nothing". For I testify again to every man that is circumcised,*

*that he is a debtor to do the whole law. The Messiah is become of no effect unto you, whosoever of you are justified by the law; ye are fallen from grace. For we through the Spirit wait for the hope of righteousness by faith. For in Yahshua the Messiah neither circumcision availeth any thing, nor uncircumcision; but faith which worketh by love".*

If Christianity had accepted that the Law of Yahweh was important to the Faith of Yahshua Messiah, the world would have treated the Jews with much more empathy and tolerance in times past.

The nation of Israel has gone through horrible experiences since 70 A.D. when Rome's war machine invaded Judea (the land of the Jews). The Roman conquest destroyed the nation, killed lots of citizens, and burnt many settlements including Jerusalem the capital city and the temple that was redesigned by Herod the King. It then took the rest of the Jewish people captives into permanent displacement. Till today as we see before our very eyes, the Jews continue to fight a great war to consolidate their sovereignty as a nation after such a long time of existing in a state of absolute powerlessness to self-determination as a group.

There is only one Perfect Living Master, one King of Kings, that is Yahshua our Messiah and this is what He says when he gave the book of revelations to the Apostle John in Revelation12:17;

*"And the dragon was wroth with the woman, and went to make war with the remnant of her seed, which keep the commandments of Yahweh, and have the testimony of Yahshua the Messiah".*

We see clearly that Yahshua Messiah is talking about the seed of a woman — a mother's offspring who kept the commandments of the Father Yahweh and the testimony of the Son Yahshua Messiah. Again, we see from the Master that Paul was in error in his attempt to set aside the Law of Yahweh. This error is now a pattern to many, especially adherents of Christianity.

Paul, in his letter to the congregation in Ephesus, wrote and introduced himself as an Apostle of Yahshua Messiah in Ephesians1:1; *"Paul, an apostle of Yahshua the Messiah by the will of Yahweh, to the saints which are at Ephesus, and to the faithful in the Messiah Yahshua:*

However, we see that in the message of Yahshua Messiah to the congregation in Ephesus through the revelation he gave to his Apostle John, the Master Yahshua Messiah states in Revelation 2:1-2;

*"Unto the angel of the assembly of <u>Ephesus</u> write; These things saith he that holdeth the seven stars in his right hand, who walketh in the midst of the seven golden candlesticks; I know thy works, and thy labour, and thy patience, and how thou canst not bear them which are evil: and thou hast tried them <u>which say they are apostles, and are not</u>, and hast <u>found them liars:</u>*

The Master indicates that there are already people who claim to be His Apostles. However, when we try them by the scriptures and by the criteria that qualifies a disciple to be an Apostle of Yahshua Messiah, we find that they do not pass the test nor meet the criteria. Therefore, their claim to be Apostles is false; hence, they are liars and imposters. We have so many of such false Apostles in Christianity today and they all have their precedence in Paul.

Meanwhile, that Paul made many errors and made a false claim to being an Apostle of Yahshua Messiah does not mean he was not a convert and did not do the work of an evangelist effectively. However, we all must know our roles in the assemblies of Yahweh in Yahshua Messiah. In knowing our roles, we should maintain and play our positions.

Yahweh is not the author of confusion. Paul himself affirmed this in his letter to the Corinthian congregation in 1 Corinthians 14:33-34;

*"For Elohim is not the author of confusion, but of peace, as in all assemblies of the saints. Let your women keep silence in the assemblies: for it is not permitted unto them to speak; but they are commanded to be under obedience, as also saith the law".*

Yahweh does not expect a woman to claim to be or play the role of a man and vice versa. We see and read in Scriptures concerning the kingdom of Judah and how Yahweh was quick to punish King Uzziah when he attempted to play the role of a priest by attempting to burn incense to Yahweh in 2 Chronicles 26:18-20;

*"And they withstood Uzziah the king, and said unto him, It appertaineth not unto thee, Uzziah, to burn incense unto Yahweh, but to the priests the sons of Aaron, that are consecrated to burn incense: go out of the sanctuary; for thou hast trespassed; neither shall it be for thine honour from Yahweh Elohim. Then Uzziah was wroth, and had a censer in his hand to burn incense: and while he was wroth with the priests, the leprosy even rose up in his forehead before the priests in the house of Yahweh, from beside the incense altar. And Azariah the chief priest, and all the priests, looked upon him, and, behold, he was leprous in his forehead, and they thrust him out from thence; yea, himself hasted also to go out, because Yahweh had smitten him".*

Also, we can glean from the rebellion of Korah in Numbers 16:28-35;

*"And Moses said, Hereby ye shall know that Yahweh hath sent me to do all these works; for I have not done them of mine own mind. If these men die the common death of all men, or if they be visited after the visitation of all men; then Yahweh hath not sent me. But if Yahweh make a new thing, and the earth open her mouth, and swallow them up, with all that appertain unto them, and they go down quick into the pit; then ye shall understand that these men have provoked Yahweh. And it came to pass, as he had made an end of speaking all these words, that the ground clave asunder that was under them: And the earth opened her mouth, and swallowed them up, and their houses, and all the men that appertained unto Korah, and all their goods. They, and all that appertained to them, went down alive into the pit, and the earth closed upon them: and they perished from among the congregation. And all Israel that were round about them fled at the cry of them: for they said, Lest the earth swallow us up also. And there came out a fire from Yahweh, and consumed the two hundred and fifty men that offered incense".*

These Scriptures are recorded for the learning and understanding of those who will later come to the Faith of Yahshua Messiah and Yahweh Elohim. Therefore, an evangelist must execute his office and not claim to be a prophet. Also, a prophet should not play the role of a pastor just for the sake of gain and honour. A woman should not play the role of a man and vice versa.

# WHY THIS WORK IS RELEVANT TODAY?

The Gospel and Faith of Yahshua Messiah is not for the believers to live a life of prosperity here on earth as taught by many False teachers in many congregations these days. The doctrine of prosperity is false and contrary to the teachings of the Master Yahshua Messiah. The Master taught his followers about giving up as many earthly possessions as possible to pursue and gain the Kingdom of Heaven. In one of the Master's teachings in Matthew 16:26, He said: ***"For what is a man profited, if he shall gain the whole world, and lose his own soul? Or what shall a man give in exchange for his soul"?***

In this verse, to "gain the world" is what we call prosperity in many teachings of nowadays preachers. In another of the teachings of the Master Yahshua Messiah, he states in Matthew 19:23-24;

***"Then said Yahshua unto his disciples, Verily I say unto you, That a rich man shall hardly enter into the kingdom of heaven. And again I say unto you, It is easier for a camel to go through the eye of a needle, than for a rich man to enter into the kingdom of Yahweh".***

In this verse, we must understand that the word <u>rich</u> represents worldly properties including cash, precious items and other assets. Meanwhile, the "rich man" represents the financially prosperous person who has gathered these worldly things.

Yahshua Messiah states in the Gospel of John in the popular verse John 3:16; ***"For Yahweh so loved the world, that he gave his only begotten Son, that whosoever believeth in him should not perish, but have everlasting life".***

Therefore, the purpose of the Faith in Yahshua Messiah is eternal life and this understanding must be read into the word of Yahshua Messiah in John 10:10; ***"The thief cometh not, but for to steal, and to kill, and to destroy: I am come that they might have life, and that they might have it <u>more abundantly</u>".***

The phrase "more abundantly" should be understood in terms of eternal life rather than in terms of worldly prosperity. Understanding it in terms of eternal life fits perfectly into the Master's teachings. On the other hand, worldly and material prosperity is contrary to the Master's teachings.

Consider a newborn baby who is healthy with normal weights and perfectly functioning organs. What kind of life is that baby born with? A good life? A normal life? An abundant life or an eternal life? Now, imagine that the child grows old, excels in his education, raises a great family, makes money, leaves a good legacy and dies at the age of 120 years. What kind of life would he have lived? Does that represent an abundant life span or a normal life span? However, if the child leaves for 1,200 years, what kind of life would that be?

Those 1,200 years will represent a very long life and abundance in years. In this analogy, the abundant life is likened to Eternal Life; it has nothing to do with material or earthly possessions. The Master teaches us in Luke 12:15; ***"And he said unto them, Take heed, and beware of covetousness: for a man's life consisteth not in the abundance of the things which he possesseth"***.

Another verse used by false apostles, false prophets and false teachers to promote their false doctrine of earthly prosperity as part of the Gospel is found in the letter of the Apostle John to a younger convert of a certain congregation by the name Gaius in 3 John 1:2; ***"Beloved, I wish above all things that thou mayest prosper and be in health, even as thy soul prospereth"***.

First of all, we observe that this is an expression of the Apostle John's wish or desire and not a doctrine. Also, we must understand exactly what the Apostle is saying when it comes to prospering. In the preceding verse, we observe what the Apostle John wrote in 3 John 1:1; ***"The elder unto the well-beloved Gaius, whom I love in <u>the Truth</u>"***.

It is obvious that the Apostle was talking about **the Truth** and wished that Gaius would **prosper** in **the Truth**, which is to <u>increase in the wisdom, knowledge and understanding of the Truth.</u> This is what it means to <u>prosper in the Truth</u> and that was what the Apostle John was wishing Gaius, along with good health. His wish had nothing to do with material or financial prosperity.

The purpose of the faith of Yahshua Messiah is **eternal life** and <u>this eternal life is with Yahshua Messiah</u>. He will give it to those who deserve it when He suddenly appears anytime soon with mighty angels and great glory. <u>No believer, apostle or prophet has been given or has received the eternal life yet.</u> That will not happen until Yahshua Messiah comes. Of course, every sincere believer of Yahshua Messiah should know that this **eternal life is the purpose of the faith.** However, the Master Yahshua Messiah made it clear that when he comes, many believers and leaders of congregations will suffer **great disappointment.** This is stated in Matthew 7:22-23;

*"Many will say to me in that day, Rabbi, Rabbi, have we not prophesied in thy name? and in thy name have cast out devils? and in thy name done many wonderful works? And then will I profess unto them, I never knew you: depart from me, ye that work iniquity".*

Why will many come to the Master upon his glorious return and claim to have done so much in the Master's name by way of heralding and proclaiming His name? Of course, they will not attempt to deceive the Master or cheat their way into his Kingdom. Rather, they are or were convinced that they were working for the Master's name. They would be disappointed by the Master's rejection.

Understanding the content of this book will save many people from this great disappointment, especially now that the Master's appearance is very close. Also, understanding the content of this book is a sure step towards accurately pinpointing the period of the Master's coming.

The Master warned His audience very seriously in Matthew 24:11; *"And many false prophets shall rise, and shall deceive many".*

The question to ask is "By what means will these many false prophets deceive so many? First, we should understand as believers that it is impossible to deceive someone with the truth. Therefore, false prophets cannot present the Truth no matter how hard they try. Hence, the Truth is the only infallible test by which to determine a false prophet. This is why the Master tells his true followers that they can identify the false prophets by their fruits. See Matthew 7:20; *"Wherefore by their fruits ye shall know them".*

However, if any believer relies on long prayers, prophecies, false miracles, lying signs and wonders as signs of authenticity of a prophet, apostle or minister, then such a person has set up himself or herself to be brainwashed and deceived by such false apostles, prophets and teachers. See Mark 13:22; *"For false Messiahs and false prophets shall rise, and shall shew signs and wonders, to seduce, if it were possible, even the elect".*

Here, the Master warns that the miracles, signs and wonders that the **'false messiahs'** which literarily means **'False anointed ones'** as we have nowadays many so-called 'highly anointed men of God' and their cohorts being false prophets busy showing and presenting signs and wonders to serve as their miracles which in turn should serve as the evidence of the authenticity of their calling and anointing, that these signs will be convincing enough to deceive everyone except the elect.

**Who is an elect?** An elect is anyone who can read this book and comprehend the content. Many believers and churchgoers cannot read and write; What chance do they stand against false prophets when they cannot read and comprehend the content of the Bible upon which their beliefs and church attendance are founded? Many can read and write but cannot thoroughly comprehend ordinary texts not to mention the Bible, a book full of parables, proverbs prophecies and dark sayings.

This situation is addressed in the prophecy of Isaiah the prophet in Isaiah 29:11-14;

*"And the vision of all is become unto you as the words of a book that is sealed, which men deliver to one that is learned, saying, Read this, I pray thee: and he saith, I cannot; for it is sealed: And the book is delivered to him that is not learned, saying, Read this, I pray thee: and he saith, I am not learned. Wherefore Yahweh said, Forasmuch as this people draw near me with their mouth, and with their lips do honour me, but have removed their heart far from me, and their fear toward me is taught by the precept of men: Therefore, behold, I will proceed to do a marvellous work among this people, even a marvellous work and a wonder: for the wisdom of*

*their wise men shall perish, and the understanding of their prudent men shall be hid"*

This is the situation in the present day Christian Church and in the ecclesia of Yahshua Messiah, including the false and genuine brethren, the true believers as well as the imposters.

This message to the Church delivered by Nathan Ben Ragshi, a prophet of Yahshua Messiah, is meant to serve as a light in the dark, and certainly the darkness cannot gainsay the revelation contained herein.

May the grace of our Lord and Saviour Yahshua Messiah of Nazareth, the Love of Yahweh Elohim and the fellowship of the Holy Spirit guide you the sincere reader to the Truth.